New and Selected Poems

NEW AND SELECTED POEMS

by Jean Garrigue

NEW YORK : *The Macmillan Company*
LONDON : *Collier–Macmillan Limited*

Library of Congress Catalog Card Number: 67-21247

FIRST PRINTING

The Macmillan Company, New York
Collier-Macmillan Canada Ltd., Toronto, Ontario

Printed in the United States of America

ACKNOWLEDGMENTS

Many of the poems in this volume were first published in magazines. The author wishes to make grateful acknowledgment to the following editors for permission to reprint these poems: *Chelsea* for "Police of the Dead Day" (which appeared originally as "Fourth Declamation"); *The Hudson Review* for "Invitation to a Hay," "Thy Love is One Thou'st Not Yet Known," "Pays Perdu," "St. Sulpice" Copyright © 1967 by The Hudson Review, Inc. and "Cracked Looking Glass" Copyright © 1967 by The Hudson Review, Inc.; *The Massachusetts Review* for "Afterwards (July 15, 1964)" from "Suite" Copyright © 1967 The Massachusetts Review; *The Nation* for "Nth Invitation" (as "Brief Letter"); *The New Republic* for "Written in London After a Protest Parade"; *The New Yorker* for "Cortège for Colette," "Amsterdam Letter," "An Improvisation on the Theme of the Lady and the Unicorn" (as "The Unicorn and the Lady"), "A Note to La Fontaine," "The Dominant House" and "Estates of the Loire"; *Poetry* for "Her Spring Song," "Flux of Autumn," Copyright © 1967 The Modern Poetry Association, "Consecration Piece" Copyright © 1967 The Modern Poetry Association, and "Little Ballad" Copyright © 1967 The Modern Poetry Association; *Poetry Northwest* for "Have Driven in Carriages" (as "Poem"), "Of a Day and Hares," "Epitaph for my Cat" and "Upon the Intimations of Love's Mortality"; *Quarterly Review of Literature* for "Again, Again" Copyright © 1967 Quarterly Review of Literature and "Of a Provincial City" Copyright © 1967 Quarterly Review of Literature; *Southern Poetry Review* for "Bleeker Street" and "Each to His Dear Keeper Gone"; *The Southern Review* for "Ballade"; *The Virginia Quarterly Review* for "A Dream," "Moon" and "The Water Wheel by the River Sorgue." The last three poems were awarded the Emily Clark Balch prize for 1966.

Contents

New Poems

FROM

Thirty-Six Poems and a Few Songs

1944

From Venice Was That Afternoon

From Venice was that afternoon
Though it was our land's canal we viewed.
There willows clove the bluish heat
By dropping leaf or two, gold green
And every tuft of hill beyond
Stood bright, distinct, as if preserved
By glass that sealed out light but not
Its gold or influence.
And floated on the speckled stream
A child of brilliant innocence
Where on the docks of green we stood
Naming it Love for its perfection.
This seemed to be . . .
But the current carried the leaves swiftly,
So flowed that child away from us,
So stared we sternly at the water's empty face.
Ah, in the greenhouse of that hour
Waited in the tare and sorrel
The mouth of fleshliness that stopped:
The leaves that dappled on that breast
The five-sensed image of our pleasance
Have now destroyed its lineaments.
For the waters of that afternoon
Flowed through Negation's glassy land
Where, in this civil, gate-closed hour
The verges of those waters now
Drown that joy that was our power.
What tyranny imposed this pride
That caused love's gift to be denied
And our destroying features to

Cast perpetually on its brow
The glass accepting no leaves now?
In rages of the intellect
We gave to heaven abstinence
Who said our love must issue from
No cisterns of the ruddy sun
But like the artifice of fountains
Leap from cold, infertile sources.
And our destroying features thus
Cast from that land its beingness
And strewed upon the green-fleshed hills
Sands of our darkening great ills.

The Stranger

Now upon this piteous year
I sit in Denmark beside the quai
And nothing that the fishers say
Or the children carrying boats
Can recall me from that place
Where sense and wish departed me
Whose very shores take on
The whiteness of anon.
For I beheld a stranger there
Who moved ahead of me
So tensile and so dancer made
That like a thief I followed her
Though my heart was so alive
I thought it equal to that beauty.
But when at last a turning came
Like the branching of a river
And I saw if she walked on
She would be gone forever,
Fear, then, so wounded me
As fell upon my ear
The voice a blind man dreams
And broke on me the smile
I dreamed as deaf men hear,
I stood there like a spy,
My tongue and eyelids taken
In such necessity.
Now upon this piteous year
The rains of Autumn fall.
Where may she be?
I suffered her to disappear

Who hunger in the prison of my fear.
That lean and brown, that stride,
That cold and melting pride,
For whom the river like a clear
Melodic line and the distant carrousel
Where lovers on their beasts of play
Rose and fell,
That wayfare where the swan adorned
With every wave and eddy
The honor of his sexual beauty,
Create her out of sorrow
That, never perishing,
Is a stately thing.

The Brook

The brook contains its landing under water.
There each leaf above is thus
Engrossed by shadows under
Nor there the stone can sunder
Filaments that make the structure.
There hang harebell's noise
Blue-peaked, and strung moss.
All is underneath the brook
Face, a building made by shadow,
No architecture of the seen
Shimmered as on earth we know.
There shades are most substantial,
Closing out the fish whose plumes
Would make beautiful,
And the sandy minnow.
But as the ambitious fly must go
Into the spider's castle
To be preservèd there
Until the castle's center
Moves upon the venturer,
So I dreamed in my buried wish
My naked senses went
That underwater's still grandeur.
I dreamed in that most glassy web
I touched with woven breast
Those galleries of glass,
Feeding invisibly on life
As insects use the membrane of the water.

The Clovers

For the heart, willing and not willing,
Is glassed under as clover in a stand of storm water.
In the downy sink of the ground
Rain is an inch deep over the heads of those four leaves
And the sides turn silver in the embossed
Pond-meadow. Think of a whole army of clover
Hidden under, lace all, green as an apple.

For the heart, willing and not willing,
Stands in a rain-settle too, transparent
To all in a vale, where the firm skin of wish
Dapples and lines it
And its veins are exposed, pale
To the tremble of world's rage, ail,
But not sky is reflected nor sun from the gray pall of heaven,
Not seed whistling by nor bird dipping.

Transparency has its savior, visible and invisible!
For as the clover stem suggests no relation
To its top parent, and under that water
Leaves stay in a stitching, sewn like a cobbled silk,
So the heart, as obscurely rooted
Is as rooted, though with a pretty way
It lies in the film of flesh, a marrow of constancy.

But nor sun reaches to nor strengthens by air
That fond delicacy
And the dwarf hidden roots, apparent to none,
Obstruct the dark muscle, a clarity upside
But a dark land thereunder,
Willing, unwilling, ignorant and imitator,
In the source of that woodland, the improvident flood.

With Glaze of Tears

With glaze of tears or of
Madness, our eyelids winged
The land: tall clouds reflected
Upon us, grass blowing in
Glint of cloud, rock, scene of
Our meetings, pathways around
The fen.
Looking into this lucid
Scene flowing beneath us, sight
Dimmed; as if the synapses
Splintered, sight darkened and failed.
For our landscape of love was
Neither each other's features
Since we were each other, but
Rich and violent country.
It was our love's and our
Soul's figuration. Now,
To stand in this separation
From cloud and flower of our kin,
Now in our seeking to close out
All spaces our eyes had run,
To know this land was symbol,
Ethereal, which had fed our veins,
Was ailing of being, was staring
To breathe flower's air or
Flower of us? Confusion trebled.
Leaping and leaping our hearts,
Sight staggered; if landscape was
Different than we, so were we,
So were we, falling, ourselves from
Ourselves cut off, emblem of love
Torn in two.

Waking, I Always Waked You Awake

Waking, I always waked you awake
As always I fell from the ledge of your arms
Into the soft sand and silt of sleep
Permitted by you awake, with your arms firm.

Waking, always I waked immediately
To the face you were when I was off sleeping,
Ribboned with sea weed or running with deer
In a valentine country of swans in the door.

Waking, always waked to the tasting of dew
As if my sleep issued tears for its loving
Waking, always waked, swimming from foam
Breathing from mountains clad in a cloud.

As waking, always waked in the health of your eyes,
Curled your leaf hair, uncovered your hands,
Good morning like birds in an innocence
Wild as the Indies we ever first found.

The Mouse

When the mouse died at night
He was all overgrown with delight,
His whiskers thick as a wood
From exploring the Polar cupboard
And his eyes still agape
From risky accomplishment.
No honor or drum was his bait.
The more glorious, he
Who with no shame for time
Then boldly died,
Three weeks a rich spell
Of sound and pure smell
And all his long leisure
For meat of short measure
(An ant could carry it.)
Praise him who sweetens
On a small hate.

Forest

There is the star bloom of the moss
And the hairy chunks of light between the conifers;
There are alleys of light where the green leads to a funeral
Down the false floor of needles.
There are rocks and boulders that jut, saw-toothed and urine-yellow.
Other stones in a field look in the distance like sheep grazing,
Grey trunk and trunklike legs and lowered head.
There are short-stemmed forests so close to the ground
You would pity a dog lost there in the spore-budding
Blackness where the sun has never struck down.
There are dying ferns that glow like a gold mine
And weeds and sumac extend the Sodom of color.
Among the divisions of stone and the fissures of branch
Lurk the abashed resentments of the ego.
Do not say this is pleasurable!
Bats, skittering on wires over the lake,
And the bug on the water, bristling in light as he measures forward his
    leaps,
The hills holding back the sun by their notched edges
(What volcanoes lie on the other side
Of heat, light, burning up even the angels)
And the mirror of forests and hills drawing nearer
Till the lake is all forests and hills made double,
Do not say this is kindly, convenient,
Warms the hands, crosses the senses with promise,
Harries our fear.
Uneasy, we bellow back at the tree frogs
And, night approaching like the entrance of a tunnel,
We would turn back and cannot, we
Surprise our natures; the woods lock us up
In the secret crimes of our intent.

FROM

The Ego and the Centaur

1947

Primer of Plato

All endeavor to be beautiful:
The loved and the loveless as well:
All women rob from duty's time
To pitch adornment to its prime.
The lion in his golden coat
Begets his joy by that; his mate
Beneath that fiery mane repeats
The fury of each sudden sense.
The swan reflecting on the stream
The opposite feathers of the swan-
Webbed dream is like the fox at night
Who glows as in original delight.
Not least, the sun in tedious round
Bestows on rock and land
Principles that all creation
Imitates in adoration.

I never knew this till I
Chanced to see how your bright cheek
Brightened from the gaze of one
Whose spirit swam a Hellespont.
I saw then that beauty was
Both for lover and beloved a feast,
The lover mirroring by his joy
That flush beauty brings, in
His eye her actual face globed small,
And beauty flattered by that glass
Pitched to its highest comeliness,
Doubled and increased until
All would seem

Derived back into first essence.
Both animals and men dwell
In such a mirror of the real
Until in sudden ecstasy
They break the boundaries of that glass
To be the image each first was.

The Mask and Knife

And I would have you clad like dominoes
In every stripe and lozenge you would dare,
A gauged discord, irregular and clair,
Or corsleted in ribands like a beau.

Be armed by shells, those profits of the Sound,
As slippered like a prince in modesty
You softly fly the docks as coarse sail cloth
Swelled by the wind and sailing bluely north.

O jacketed like jockeys in a silk!
I'd have you rayed and tangled in douce ropes
Where hawsers found their ships at captive ports.
Odor of fur, a belle cool din!

Till when the shock of some dark pose
Makes leapt commotion like a white furore
Of one wave, only one wave seen
Raging on the night-paned seas

Or as the Spring unwinds the flood
Or as a perfume galls the scrupled blood
And you have yoked me till I cannot break
Though broken I as uncouth horsemen might

Bully a spirit to its brink.
And your very name—its lips make weights in me.

Old Haven

Directions that you took
Which told me how I could
Amid those cultured streets describe
My rude impulse to you,
Now turn within my head,
Signs tangled while I sought
Good milkmen who could set me straight.

As those on bicycles
Who asked me was I lost
And moldy houses that concurred
With cornices to bless,
All proved such lesson of
Love's reassuring depths.

The churches of the place
And dear, pastured squares
Like museum objects borrowed
An ancient air to please
Till dim old gentlemen
Like robin goodmen winked
And sprightly dogs were unicorns.

Now absent from you, dear,
My fatuous joy declares
How love may change a city, give
Glee to horses pulling
Loads, to gutters virtue
And to salesmen, grace.

For smile so sweetly those
Tottering cupolas, old
Curbs in my enamored thought (where
Spongy Florida steals
The stale New England air),
I ponder on love's strength,

So cunning when direct,
So roguish when sincere!
If dogs may charm because you're there,
Drugstores infatuate,
And meanest citizens
Like saints from niches step
To guide me to your goodness and to luck.

Poem

I saw the mountains in a rose-fire light
Upon my ill-housed street, whose old-law flats
Were stained a blood light, rose-christ light.
Those mountains of the sun I saw,

All peaked and small, like waves that stabilize
Their pearl, or crystallize into a snow
Their light, all cast aboundingly from out
The fiery brim, the golden den of night.

As if a skiey flame could crucify
Our lives, the prisons of conceptual plight,
I saw, I wept, for we were all burning,
Our faces all, in crucibles of light.

Immutable vision of the beautiful
That changes once and once again with light!
A cloud cast on the sun its ire,
That flaming and descending sun did then depart
And it was gray, the first of night.

I saw how easily we start—
Our hearts in us that so desire the fire
I saw and wept and we were all.
I saw and wept, my cheek did burn

Vision and illusion, Oh return!
That I with joy and fire and light
In fire and light and delicate joy my life
May live in crucibles like that, and burn.

Only the Irresistible Abides

At the crossing, wind-stricken in blow, I saw
Him of dead cares in penal fire.
The wind foully fell; the dung of the bird dropped.

Rough was the blast; rough clove bones to the beat
Flesh in such charge, shift.
Leaves drove backwards and forwards,
The horse reared; in the near distance sheep nudged,
Seeking determination of their warmth.

Crying aloud, my voice was snatched
Only to be tossed high like a leaf, empty
The word returned to my struck mouth.
Clearly going into my heart, had rolled back
His brow from its torment, his eyes from their penance.
What matter, cry of the wind hissing,
Sucking his face?
To my heart I trembled as radically changed the nature of him,
Spoliation, the bitter air of corruption.
Foresaw strength devoured by the weakness it came forth from,
The eye, flag of the war,
Dark light of the head, dark, hovered blood,
Cut tear, maniacal pity,
The smile bled by its subtleties there,
Killed pang, satirical mercy,
Sleep dead; the mouth closed like a grave upon
Traitorous censors, sweet frauds, hypocrites of the heart.

We passed; breath torn, bleeding,
I was at raw rock, dark the pit, roaring.

Foresaw his daemons with whom he contended,
Foresaw his battle running against him,
For the delicate conscience alone has embraced defeat,
Saw in spite of the issue always in question,
His lion-like labor.

Love, like those shadowy starlings wailing,
Plunged against buildings, their blind bodies falling,
Love, born to my breast, rose, more rugged
Than gust, blast, instructing his tyrants,
Of his abyss defiant,
Courier caught sweet blood of his tears, sweet anguish wrung,
As his name I came to through valleys of evil, of honor
Resisting no evil nor knowledge that the soul endeavor
World in him.

Song

O beautiful, my relic bone,
Whitening like the foreign moon,
Whose luster consummates my tomb.

O beautiful, my flesh rose-grown,
Rose-rose white from that small bone
Whose vapor is the breath I own

And tendrils of my blood curl in.
Rose-rose white, the flesh I am
But murderer eye and murdered!

For all the flesh becomes an eye:
I am no flesh while yet eye's eaten
The rose-rose flesh bare to the bone,

Bare to the bone! But that flesh still
By heat of dews renews again.

O bless, occurrence of the moon
When actual flesh of both is gone,
My flesh the air the eye takes in,

That flesh on bone the air the eye takes in,
Death-wedding the moon shines in.

False Country of the Zoo

We are large with pity, slow and awkward
In the false country of the zoo.
For the beasts our hearts turn over and sigh,
With the gazelle we long to look eye to eye,
Laughter at the stumbling, southern giraffes
Urges our anger, righteous despair.
As the hartebeest plunges, giddy, eccentric,
From out of the courtyard into his stall,
We long to seize his forehead's steep horns
Which are like the staves of a lyre.
Fleeter than greyhounds the hartebeest
Long-muzzled, small-footed, and shy.
Another runner, the emu, is even better
At kicking. Oh, the coarse chicken feet
Of this bird reputed a fossil!
His body, deep as a table,
Droops gracelessly downwise,
His small head shakes like an old woman's eye.
The emu, the ostrich, the cassowary
Continue to go on living their lives
In conditions unnatural to them
And in relations most strange
Remain the same.
As for the secretary bird,
Snake-killer, he suggests
A mischievous bird-maker.
Like a long-legged boy in short pants
He runs teetering, legs far apart,
On his toes, part gasping girl.
What thought him up, this creature

Eminently equipped by his nervous habits
To kill venomous snakes with his strong
Horny feet, first jumping on them
And then leaping away?
At the reptile and monkey houses
Crowds gather to enjoy the ugly
But mock the kangaroo who walks like a cripple.

In the false country of the zoo,
Where Africa is well represented
By Australia,
The emu, the ostrich and cassowary
Survive like kings, poor antiquated strays,
Deceased in all but vestiges,
Who did not have to change, preserved
In their peculiarities by rifts,
From emigration barred.
Now melancholy, like old continents
Unmodified and discontinued, they
Remain by some discreet permission
Like older souls too painfully handicapped.
Running birds who cannot fly,
Whose virtue is their liability,
Whose stubborn very resistance is their sorrow.
See, as they run, how we laugh
At the primitive, relic procedure.

In the false country of the zoo
Grief is well represented there
By those continents of the odd

And outmoded, Africa and Australia.
Sensation is foremost at a zoo—
The sensation of gaping at the particular:
The striped and camouflaged,
The bear, wallowing in his anger,
The humid tiger wading in a pool.
As for those imports
From Java and India,
The pale, virginal peafowl,
The stork, cracking his bill against a wall,
The peacock, plumes up, though he walks as if weighted
—All that unconscionable tapestry—
Till a wind blows the source of his pride
And it becomes his embarrassment,
The eye, plunged in sensation, closes.
Thought seizes the image. This shrieking
Jungle of spot, stripe, orange
Blurs. The oil from the deer's eye
That streaks like a tear his cheek
Seems like a tear, is, is,
As our love and our pity are, are.

FROM

The Monument Rose

1953

The Opera of the Heart: Overture

Music at this, and now the kings throw dice
Or favor your wild beauty by that sky
They know the gods appareled white with stars
Who stung and pale, indifferent as those maps you rule,
Are then appointed by our passioned wills, know you?
To mysteries more savage than you cry
When pavilioned, we send you on those ways
Our jewels fall upon, the cutting cost
We rake from out our hearts to give to you.

Music at this, till when you laugh
That's then a scar of shock upon our eyes.
You fling against us, break, we see
All that we shrink from, cast on you
And all its stain blood-sick, and see you go
From dancing, say, to dark rooms of the soul
From which all music's closed although it comes
In gusts like dying leaves whose odor is
A flask of virile sweetness saturate with
The agony of fresh-had wounds in us.

Or then that overtowers us like a far concourse
Trembling and hasting with a heaven's rage.
The kings dare not, the gods withdraw their siege.
There stir in the dressing room those shades
That search your exile with their lolling hands
Drugged with the smoke-fat torch their cerements
Although you move as though you played a game
More sensual than the wish of multitudes.
It draws us after you like crows or dogs
Tasting a wintry death that fires the blood.

And yet, our swan, who at the instant rise
Daring in flood those great steps of the heart
And, when the action's come, so mount on it
You'd think traducers of its monumental white
Dared death to the empress snows your sceptre strikes,
Though in the dark it seems you're orphaned still,
Or that the slumbering child who mothers you
Still cried the moon up clangorous night
When your half-look which visits now our hearts
Must veil your own from us and this white thing.

Music at this, until the sky rolls drums
And you for whom the tear-hung flowers fall
From arms disarmed or fire-flung, cluster still,
Mobbed with the tariffs of that wine-rich tone
Our ceremonial fevers till with plume
And counterpane and silk you take the map
Eluded that we bent on in the light
Stabbing its red and green with graven sight.

Queen of that other country, our own beast!
All that you do comes out of such a dark,
Your subtle blood so brooding and so taught
By powers borne from out the abyss to us
And from disease its beauty, youth its wraith,
It shames the heart! Till worldless now a world
We see you go toward what in an instant
Flames up like a star, and odors in their blowing leaves
Blow with the weight of old eternities,
And you survive our care like infant gods.

The Strike of the Night

Fate, heat, the strike of the night,
It is all seen inward in time.
We love what we love for ill or good
It is the fascination of what is done
And we are blood, blood
Moves in the mind. Is it blind, blind?
Is as well, wine. Is it doom? As much
Song. And the night plucks open our veins,
Strong, strong.

In the garden the roses scattered
When under the wickets I came
To their blooming there on the mound.
Such early largesse of red
Succeeding the flags overthrown.
Bees rolling in golden cups
And the Persian wine of those pinks
Crossing the sense with their powders, oils
To be pressed in the prime
Of the year's still white and green
Till I saw a wreath cast down.
There, what a spectre tomb!
In the shape of the dwindled moon.

For all the unborn, it sang, a song.
For those who are about to die, another
One. A song or son, laughed the worm.

There was into the nights this blood
Slaughtered by seasons, the pent-up fume

Dislodging its petals one by one
In the liquefaction of June.

But I was in the pale of the wood
Before I saw what I understood
And after, at the door of the west
Before there struck and clanged my breast.

Gravepiece

It is there where the worm has egress
That I prod these bones in their lair
And would push them out of their proper place
To find the vivid core

The heart I pried from the worm's small jaws
When I spied the nail
And its intricate system of holding down the dead
Who weary of the grave's moist hell

Now other than the worm may pulp and tear
For I threw it out of its grinning clothes
It is my heart that runs among these bones
And the virid excess of the enormous hair

In the dead of night the dogs that had the heart
To seize the heart I threw (and rived the air)
Will come with the mangled thing afire on their tongues
And find me out where I stacked the bones

And made a crosstree from the thigh's long ones
Such fire will burst my swound in a shift of bones
Crippled with one for a crutch I will come forth
In the dead of night the dogs will find us both

We will hang on the cross and chatter of love in the winds.

The Maimed Grasshopper Speaks Up

I have three simple eyes
Perceiving love, death, and hate
Up close, as insects do,
Who thrive by the particular view.

The biggest eyes, with armor on,
That gave me fore and backward sight
Into the ditches of rash thought
Serve me not, the armor's broke.

Thus I may not leap which way
Into the truths of enemy
Or love's fool's ruddy cave
Or the inscrutable world's vault

Lest the rude, simple feelers break.
Thought asks for eyes that see all round
And make its parts to jump the moon,
Monument leapers, leopards of intellect.

Universalists of sight,
I to that moon am like the blind
Who may but feel, not see its light.
And thus in destitution sit.

World without end, commend me to your might
That I my simple eyes may set
On it, or death, or hate, and get some light.

Invocation to Old Windylocks

That blue, that dark, dark, green-dark blue,
That knolled dome and cone, magnetic sphere
Whose rough-edged line's an adamant composed
By this sheer falling of the world's line here
Of continents, the clouds, now mapped and cloven,
Breast, cleft, and magnanimities
Whose boughs are earth, whose earth is air,
Air, light, that blue, that dark, dark, green-dark blue
And weight, whose dark sides trammel me

That blue, that dark, dark, green-dark blue
By this mid-sunlight pierced whose shafts and rifts
From delicate armories thinned do bend
Across the dredged green crest:
Wave steadfast, graven in the unstained clear
Refractive of the earth's rapt atmosphere—
Paladin rim-foiled, centurion
Of the untrodden distance, suspiration of stars,
Whose gaze now holds us, fixed and pierced,
To this obstacle's strict post
The energy of our unearthly hopes!—
That is dark-blue, that is dark-green blue,
Flesh of timber wrung through
As lilac enflasked in its smoky color
Gives up on the white alphabet of the river—

That is dark-blue, that is dark-green blue
Upon whose edge the sunlight falls and swifts
Exhumed, say, from a dark crop of violets,
Intricate outlaying embased

Upon the blue and white enfolded
Of the very centuries impounded
That at the tag-ends of such space—

Thy steeps and falls, thy rigor
Curled, pressing out of the world,
Where not even the bee stings
Though the wind wallows in troughs of cloud
Winking like leaves whose tops are similar nests—

Configuration of weight, heat, energy
Anchoring the sky in exhalations almighty
Thy stroked slopes and downs,
Thy amorous sides enshaped by air,
In the perspectives of hailed eternity!

By the sworn vapors where we turn
Turned, falling, to fall upon
When by optic we tremble at the cliff,
Pock-marks of the delirious distance
As if from a cloud! we rode, the eye
Astride its surface on a reined-out wind—

If to look were to touch, move, be.
Perspective in thy light as to
In the revolutions of ecstasy
Precipitate that green, that dark elixir

And in the sharp wood and shadow
Inverted upon thy pastures

To go all up and down, to embrace thee,
Traversed, translucent slopes, or bird-gods we
To thy light's four round declivities—

Night birth of cloud, to be
In the delirium of mists or thy clear sea—
Diamond cast forth from the earth's rage,
Rarefied arrogance beside whom
The clear star rests and reigns,
Deep in the midsummer casque of flesh
Exalted, secret, calm, and vast, to stay—
Into which the night clambers and the day—
Thicket entangled, up which in ropy ascent
Vapors in the clear fervors of morning rest
Like a mid-Norway

And we held to thee, infatuate on thy flank
Great prow, aerial bulk,
Florilegium, stepping forth into fresh-running light,
Arcana coelestia.

For Anybody's Martyr's Song

What's love that's always strong?
Beasts from the Antipodes, spring down!
And hoydens leap like lions over beaches!
Love is the friend whose faithfulness is wit,
Is best your mimic when you tongue-tied vow,
Aloof when you win and surly when you stammer,
Cries I do not understand you, and
Corrects your right answer.

Indulges with contempt your sweet tooth at the fair,
Gives you fearful rides on the roller coaster,
Greets you like a sovereign when you've come
An hour, but puts the green toad in your bed
Just as soon thereafter.
Your sober love turns tomcat in the bar.

Children hate school, soldiers discipline,
Love hates love but what's the good of that?
O the sweet cry, the dark eye!
Love stamps its foot but cannot slip the knot.

Nor can remove the leopard's spot
Nor ever dye the wolf white,
Love loves what love is
Nor can it change that.

Address to the Migrations

A pounding on wood. The woodpecker.
The turfed castle of ants. The weeds very still.
It is autumn and I lie on the ground
In the thin pelt of the sun.
The sky is low and sealed around
With doors and walls of clouds rippled like shells.
Autumnal whiteness thins and rarefies,
I lie in the strawy wood and close my eyes.
All would be silent but that pods
Break and seeds let go.
A burring of wings in papery weeds.
I would sleep in the sling of autumn till white snow
Sifted and fulfilled its dying saws
Of insects pitching and leaping at wild doors.
And sumptuary laws. Suspension of stillness
While there draws, flying and lighting,
Streamers of seeds.
A chill befalls me when they fall.
By death? By death? In the henna fields?
Or sleepy death preparing his long mills?
Suddenly all over the fields a barking of crows.
While far above, it seems, a strangeness sails
Or delicate strangeness calls. It is not to be heard.
These are imagined cries.
And I awake to go and turn and rise.
There is a black thread in the skies
Notched like an arrow and it streams from clouds.
Peaks let it go.
Now wind to wind the sky is filled with some
Tremor and echo, intervals

Staying and falling you cannot hear—
Bugled communion! panging up the air
Or already flight is so fast flight pangs the ear.
The line comes near, thin as a hair
And some fly there back of its prow
And some fly riffling the shaft's seamed edge that reams the air
Till the sky seems cut and clouds part there
Or is it air raveling these ranks? It pulls faster
Till on the wheel of some vast round veers left.
The stook of the sun stands here and further walls.
One instant more and it has plunged past, gone—
Door beyond door, leaving the whole sky-rift,
Atlantic vistas, depthless drifts beyond drifts.
Now lumber up and would flop after, crows
Like spies the country wished of rearguard thought,
Loosed feathers from the shaft that drove.
My turfed castle of ants is busy . . .

Line, sign, glyph out of time,
Ancestries of language riding, this writing,
Once on the pearly beachhead of the day
We saw you there.
Animal ravings towered the air. Hounds
And the tame birds bayed and clapped their claws
And I, I hailed and cried
Some divination yielding up its laws
Nor know I line of music or of words
Sent from the shaft more perfectly across
This body of the world than that brief race
Seen for an instant there in the immense.

Lightly Like Music Running

Lightly like music running, our blood
In the darling dogdays of early youth,
We nimbled with vines, ferns were cast over
The limpid lip of the sky, moistness we clambered.
This was the sun come dandling down
Green Babylon in the thronged sheaves—
Shelled such dingles, tan such bloom
By the roved brooksides, all the day long.
Lightly like music running, our blood
In and out of the cloud's woven pastures,
It was all in the shade of the vines and meadows
Where Adam delves, in the green fables
Of the dogdays, in early youth.

This Day Is Not Like That Day

This day is not like that day.
That was a day majestic with clouds,
Barrows of fruit, ices, and birds,
And in the pink stalls the melon,
While the mango, magniloquent stem,
Steeped him in baskets, Othello's green,
And there were strawberries, the plums and the figs.
This day is not.

That was a day when forth from the farms
The winds, pale as straw, were in mounds
Heaped like green hay freshly torn from ground.
Then did the air thrust so cleanly in leaves
Their delicate fans beat long.
In the water, rings of the sun ran.

And in the skies, the snows
Traveling by feckless shores
Shed forth from their pallid moors
The obscure moon stains of the night
Or those curds of light at the top
From the fissured sides and deep cavern rent
Of the tentless mountains, our guards.

It was a day of gods—sweet provisions
From the wine realm! tournaments!
Castles! our wondering psalms
Bearing up day to its summits day long!
Which now in its dustfall time
Sifts. The attraction

Of stone to stone pulls at the road,
Clouds thin and tear into nothing.

Patience and faith, my heart!
All urns are gathered in dark
With leaves that sang in the sun
Of some rapt mind burning long
In its visions, which vanishèd.

There Is a Dark River

There is a dark river flows under a bridge
Making an elbowed turn where the swallows skim
Indescribably dark in rain.
You think of the Floss, drifting down
To the boyhood of the implacable maelstrom
And a boathouse rotting in shadow.
The grapes of Concord are thick with hawthorn
And the old manse is ripe with the eaved rain.

There is a dark river under a bridge
Where beyond, grasses stand up
Most English lone at the wide bend.
Those oblivion-haunted ones who wrote
Memorable words on the window pane,
What but the diamond's firmness gives them name?
And yet because they did it
The field is thick with spirit.

Across from this rich running a crop
Under the pines of black-toothed stones.
Happy the lilacs; happy each stem
By the troughs of the green sunk down.
Something other than animal dread
Made us pray when we stood by them
That this same love with the full of thought
Go down and touch at the base of the root
The unutterable, which is unmortal.

There is a dark river flows under a bridge
Where the reeds stand in the come and go
Of a boathouse black in the shadow.

Here swallows fly over its swirl.
A wild gyre of midges below.
There by the tremble of water
Spectres whom we might know
Stand chanting of what we no longer
May read the text for, in the shadow.

And yet the color of their tears is over the water
And the air is plunged into echo
Of their long eyes in the mirror.
Do we not see this, do we not know—
There in the gliding below
Is not the sight slanted with thought
Of this same willow from which they drank.

Rich-running water, indescribably much
Emblackened by wild-running years
As at nightfall when clamor thickens
All the night over with sleeping things,
Invisible footfalls and murmurings—

Here where the swallows drink from the bend
Shadows our shadows stir
In the trepidation of light
That the down-reaching boughs collect
Ah! To feel is to understand
Here in the to and fro
Of what looks forth and what glides over
How all might recur again,
So rich the tremble there seems to wed
Kingdoms of flesh and shade.

A Water Walk by Villa d' Este

1959

One for the Roses

My dancing roses, dancing in November,
Your red more deepened for the sun has waned,
The frost is black on the grass, green-gray the ice,
And still within this court you dance.

And yet your petals toughened by the cold,
Bowed in the grass like small-clothes dropped,
The bud most champfered where the cheek was rich
As mildest infants in their sleep of lace,

My dancing roses, dancing in November,
Parterre, parlance, my rose plantation,
When winds that start the hectic sting and chill,
Pierce me with thorns still pliant and still green

Though fallen is the nest and honeycomb,
That butterfly, it barely fans the light,
And numb the wasp, the bee drowsy
Though still serene, half-rapt

Because he's near his parcels yet
Of providences left,
If I be not the witness of your reign,
Your scarlet like a vintage the decree

Your fallen petals now its seal
To undertake as faithfuls do, the fire
Of how you flourish on the year's deathbed.
So, temperate queens, upon that sighing-out

There on the short cold grass when wind has come
Up to your green-hinged knees and snow has blown
Those lovely crowns you wore the half-year long,
To spurn with your valor, and by red singe white.

Not that I seek the moral, rose,
Nor preach to you from rostrums, dear,
Whose dial marks the umbering of the year,
But that the way you stain and dye the air

Banked with the hedgerow of the plum and gold
Is peerless, and more mad than ruin.
To walk among your tiers where the dew is cold,
Your damson signet and your green my rule,

As, on that morning when the wind comes
Blowing a cloud of snow up to your leaves
And crowns on whom the wind expounds, to say:
I have beheld you in your dominion, rose,

And you are light and day.

A Garland of Trumpets

That festival day by the sea
There was such light-bannered gaiety
I walked resting in it, it passed me
Like figures drawn in a dream.
A mountain soft-rising in earth flesh
Green and deep-tracked, and water
A daylight color, all mountain drenched
In the blue of it, and green grottoes,
And those wild youths on the breakwater
Picnicking out the day
What but commotion their revelry,
While a small cart struggles up the street
And a painted cart rolls by,
High-stepping horses plumed and dressed.
Not Bacchus' lolling, paw-soft beasts
Could be more gay.
Held, beheld all in a dream,
The fishermen dark as the sea,
Foam-dappled, wading the shallows
Clear to transparency,
Lightly driving their boats out to sea.
Held, beheld all, as one gazes
Out of a storm-laden window.
Wind vexing clouds, blowing moistures to flowers,
Vendors heaving up over sea walls,
Wheels racing by from which streamers fly,
Cockades, pompoms, while the great gay hours
Go with the sails riding out white as moths
On the blue-masted air of the bay.
Cart day. Band day. Easter after.

All day this riding and feasting.
A praising, a spirit excelling,
A garland of trumpets beating with gold
The tired god up from his sleep
That festival day by the sea.

A Mourning
(FOR DYLAN THOMAS)

The day was unbearably mild
When he went forth in his clothes
Tears of his mother had spent
She sowed with her leaping woe

And the rage of her bloody rent.
Bare of the garments reft
In the costume of water he went
Crushed by the sacrament

Of the heavy blood he had lent.
Unbearably mild was the day
A quarreling of bells in the sky
Delicately the fountains gave

The jet of the living waters to eyes.
Forth from all this walked he
In a language foreign to us
Transparently back into earth.

Did we see him or think we did
Back from his jaunting journey
To the keep and its dark plot early?
Heartbreakingly mild the day

A mystery of flowers in the sky . . .

    II
O where is that mirth and furore
Worked by his casting lords

When he paced the shift of the sea cold side
In his mirage-beholding blood?

Nothing that did not have a voice
In the coils of his veins and salt
When he wound forth like a sailor crooked
By a snail-backed hump of net

And unraveled his whole soul's pack
Down the winding thread to the knot
By patched and knit and unknit web
To skein all origin out.

Or strapped to wings when he went
To call his towers in a cloud
Nothing but did not there abound
In the dissembling element

When Merlin of sails and Perseus
On a beast's back he stood and struck,
Ghost-sieging kiss and lineament
By rack and rein and line to get

For an emblem in a shroud.
O where is that mirth and furore?
Let the birds hush and the clouds stop
Their restless building on battlements

That we saw him drawn down
By the water-doused and wind-shaking dark—

Agape birds by his trident cries—
To the musing source where he lies.

III
Unbearably mild was the day
When he went forth in his clothes.
In the foreign skies of our flowers
The headlong bells bay out.

A panging of bells in the wind
For the one death over again
And clouds that the birds run to
From the sky that the bells tear out.

Bear bells your grief away
Bear bells that breaking bay
When he went forth in his mother's clothes
In the leap of tears to the vault.

Bear bells that cracked love bolt
Forth on water and light
To drive with the birds and the cloudshot towers
Through the gay transfiguring night.

A Figure for J. V. Meer

She who weighs pearls, who plays lutes
By the crimson rug on a table,
By the chair with lions reared on its back
Standing, posed, facing the full fall of light
There over her left shoulder,
Or interrupted at music, or clasping a book
In a yellow jacket bordered by ermine,
Or in a blue robe, leaves far voluted the color of blue
In her hair,
In her hand the slender gold trumpet,
By a sloping dish, a peach divided in half,
By the spinet marbled in brown, gray, and black,
Gray and gold the checkerwork of the floor,
Stilled standing there in a mesh
Of the movement of light on light
As fixed it would genuflect
On the studs of the chair,
On a pearl in the ear,
Silks on the wall, maps, ewers, and globes
And waiting stilled there
Lifting up to the eyes of the server
Mouth bemused, a sweetness resting there
As if from some inward air,
Steps in the soul or what
All attention must bend to hear
Bliss like a tempering messenger . . .

And the blue velvet chair, the spinet or virginals,
The letter, a wineglass that covers the mouth,
The viola upon its back and a lute

Or the page of music by the gilt frame—
Allusions and scriptless emblems
Like the fish or the peacock or vine,
Signs for the ungiven thing
She converses with on that light gathering in.
And whoever she is standing there
About to play music or hear
From that server who bears foretellingly
Measures into a chamber
The clairvoyance of lemon made northern by amber,
A sense of some brimming raised in a cup . . .
As if deep back in the interior
Enclosed by the coffered rim
Gildings from the illuminations,
Figures in gold-leaf flame,
Returned through translucence again
Atomies of the passion,
A vial of roses and blood.
Like a clarity of being become
A concordance, an equation, this light
With the soul transformed in its chamber.

A Demon Came to Me

A demon came to me in love's disguise,
One of the lower order of hell's guard,
The devil's angel, as it once was coined,
Cool as marble, with a heart like iron.
I could not see it then, the demon smiled
And past experience warned but would not prove.
Besides, the fellow was so very proud,
Immaculate in blackness like a god,
And rife with Adam's ruddy vainglory.
This angel, arrogant of life, swore love.
I, casting off the weight of my short past,
Swore truth was half in novelty's red chance,
And thus in his squat cage I basked.
Foul was fair and fair was foul, confess!
To such confusion have I paid betimes.
Who loves his demon fears his life,
Who loves his pain denies his god.

Dialog in the Dark Tower

O where lies that land
And the enormous heat of its brilliant skies?
"There, there, in those eyes,
There's where it lies."

O how may I find it now?
An evil spirit closed
That landscape off from me.
"Pray to the souls who bid his angels rise."

And if I do? White morning comes and dies
That vision when it seemed he came
With killed love back and mercy in his eyes.
"Forget! Forgive!"

That perfidy and guise
As love to love takes when it strikes?
"The wound we suckle hates us next to death!"
But who pretends forgiveness is as cracked—

To practice gay hypocrisy to kill—
The crime he practiced when he kissed,
Strict as a serpent in his vengefulness.
"O child, I fear you never will again

Behold those cloudlands and their skies.
Lost they are to your own eyes.
Look to your heart. Its dark invades
What will increase its lot by every vise

Poison or madness quite as kind
For hate obtains a marble of the mind
Sense boils in ice, the eyes go iron.
It is that petrifaction by the wound

Unless, as though it were your own,
Mercy he took you give on every hand
And go to the rose and eat of it,
Put delicate stuff of crystal at your sight,

Forgiving rise, forgiving sink by that."
The natural sun! The natural light!
If I were wise. But I am not.
And knowledge is not gained at every sense

Nor wisdom supped from every vat.
"Not wisdom but deliverance is your goal."
Pride scorns such mouthings to the soul!
"Then suffer hell for that!"

Why, hell's a hell we must get at.
"God pity you."
Say not, for I will see to it.

One Third of a Dream

When was I scalloped with leaves,
When was my body half horse
When in the fields where the gods race
At sports with bugle and lance
Did I have as companion the eagle-beaked griffon,
Fringed hair down his throat and his body?

Was it other than I who tied the animal claws about me
And wore over my head the beast-friend mouth,
Open the tigrish jaws for me to stare through,
Given the dual-headed look?

Languors of flesh and stone—the stripling god
Leaning against a bough, his lyre before him,
And meads of the blue-veined water, dimpled and tented,
A stretch of the sky beside land. . . .

This Swallows' Empire

Wrought by the odd desire for permanence
I'd hammer down that barn's boards one by one
The ivy's nudged apart and winds have sprung
And icy blows and summer's pounding suns.
Those gaping windows, too, and half-cracked panes,
The door that broke from its hinges leans against
The blackened exit mouth, and all such things
As let the rude rot in and thieving rain
I'd be so prompt to take defense against
And fortify and make so sound
You'd think it'd haunt me on some howling night
When all seems waste unless I could
To all that trouble say: this much will stand,
This swallows' empire for a little while
And bolts of hay in their warm cave
And drifts of straw upon the broad-beamed floor.
Though time must turn all waters for its mill
And nothing is but grist as we well know
What has withstood two hundred years
That rich resistance will do so
If obdurate work allows, for fifty more
For fifty more to house the hay
They cut and pile in stripèd rows
And will carry in before the sun's flower goes.

As if within this shelter here
For what the toppling wagons bring
From ricks in fields to fill the loft
With rustling fragrance and with warmth
There might be some more delicate thing

Dozing in some attic in some spring
That shafts in through the windows in a dream
Of meadows in their prime unreaped, uncut,
Unreaped, uncut, and running with the wind—
The golden burn, the darksome gold or green.
Pressed to the rafters all that airy weight
And caught within, now looking out,
Past time's compulsions in the massy dark,
Their golden heads and stalks of light.
I mean those summers of the foursquare fields
That memory, by its strange persuasion yields,
And blazoning, from dim abandonment.

For the Fountains and Fountaineers
of Villa d'Este

Say that these are the fireworks of water,
One hundred fountains on the tiers of plains;
That goddesses enthroned hold spears of it,
It erupts from the mouths of shagged eagles,
And moss-legged gods, one side of the face worn off by it,
Straddle the silver, unmitigated flood.
Say that the down play and up play
And fourteen shafts around a central plume
Not to discount the dragons spouting it
That meet two dolphins plunged in it
Sending their streams against the contending ones,
Are a continuum in a series of play by water
And play by light on the water, making arcs
Of a spectrum in the din and bafflement
Of that most muffled watery bell beat, pell mell and lulled stampede,
So that an insatiable thirst
Cannot be allayed in the blood.
Though they flow round the very bones,
Though a tumult of vapor rising from them
Blows the leaves of the tree by their weight,
Nothing, no, not by any rain-making vows.
Nor any meandering of boughs
Down the stone-flagged paths and the avenues
Of the serpentine oleander
Whose branch knots and slippering leaves
Knit such a shade in the place of green light
It is a scandal of pleasure,
Say that nothing, no limestone grotto alive
With the sibylline god gushing forth

This silver, non-potable liquid,
Can convey to the fever coolness
Nor a slaking, a quenching by dews
Where the scent of the water buds.

Here are fans of water, and silver combs,
Peacock-eyed in the sun-glints upon them,
Vines and wreaths trailed round a stone,
And thirst has become a delirium,
It heaps on the brain,
It plunges along the arm,
In a sleep by leaves
It buries half the blood.
Taking one sinuous course down the breast
It would thrust and lock round the heart in a trice.

While, to stand, sheathed in a grotto
On the reverse side of this shield of water,
Downpouring in pound on pound
Its chafed, silver-shot metal . . .
I know of no fury that tells
More to me, deafening, than that
Of a velocity past which I'd know
Nothing but the hurl and fall
Of those burst rockets of water
Driving their sweetness into the ground
In a blaze of lightnings and stars
As in wet dusts shattering on stone
To explode with soft fury again.

Shield of the water and water wall,
Water roots, tentacles, bars,
Spears of water and bolts,
I know nothing here but the sense
In this downflowing fall
Of the wilderness of eternity.
And I am flailed to earth.
I am dank as a river god.
Scallop on scallop of the primeval flat water leaf
With no roots but in water, taking its substance from liquid,
Coats me and jackets me over.
I am dense as lichen,
Primordial as fern,
Or, like that tree split at its base,
Covert for winter creatures and water-retreated life,
Tip with my boughs very serpent green,
Or in a grand spirit of play
Spurt water out of my nostrils.

Veins and gaddings of water,
I have seen you in a fall
Shoot madness into a marble,
And ever the thud and *pronk* of the pump,
Hee-haw and frog *harrumph!*, that heave and rail
Of the mechanical works
That create the genius of water flowing . . .

To tread the crests of the fountains,
To walk on the foam of their flowers,
Upthrust in a vertical climbing
Spires of the falling and changing stuff

In a ghost play of dance
Creating beyond their climbing
Caps of their vapor, a white turbulence
Of that which so changes beyond them
It is sur-foam, surf-combed,
It is got by the mathematics of climbing—
To reach by those aerobatics into white snows of the mounting—
There to dissolve into
What brings all the condensed fury of dews
Back down into descending.

To dance on those heavy heads of water
So richly and artfully sustained
By white prongs and tongues of the air
Curdling up liquid from nowhere,
The advance and the sword of a watery swirl
That is somehow compact with air,
Or to take from the lull
Of the deep music such a dream
As will not abandon flame,
To sink into the deep-blown
Horn-called music and the wind-
Flung and cheek-puffed
Surge and hee-ho-hum of the thing . . .
Shagged eagles that do not spout
By *fleur de lys*, all moss, that do,
And the shafts then and the boat-shaped urn—
Three kinds of shapes of water flowing
Across two kinds of spouts descending
And one out of the mouths of horned or big-eared animal gods.

A water walk by all this bewildering
Fantasy of arising and falling flutes of the water,
Columned water adorned, making a gush and warble of sound.

II
Fountains, if to behold you
Were to have rain down over me
The least tendril and slightest shoot
Of your very white jubilation!
In the coil of your spirits be wound!
Or wrapped in your sleek skins
Mortality itself unfitted,
Made wild as it was, bound in rings
Of the lightly springing-up streams
That go in a series of crystal hoops
And twenty such hoops you have,
Twenty wickets of running light
In glittering slivers of it
Set in an *Alice* water garden
Where the cultivation is water, not earth,
Stamens and stems of water stuff,
Emblems of water pouring from emblems,
Griffons that jut it, like merry she-gods
Winged at the back but firm fish-tailed
From whose breasts spurt the magnificent jets!

As I beheld you down levels of grass,
Throwing out the wild mists of forgetfulness.
Gashing down through the tender grace
Of a green confinement by slopes.

White channels were a most beautiful thing,
Channels, chalk white, with the sluice's spume
Were a most beautiful, astonishing thing
Coursing with mad dog race down the grass
From one fountainous place to the next.
As I saw you in bird-frail seines
Down a green depth of height.
Sinews and locks fine as veils
Showing all vegetation behind them,
Chains, flashing and weaving,
Strands as of links of snow
Released and transformed into air.
Below, a deep chasm, a tangled abyss
Only a bird may sift, flying down the crevasse
For a sip from a luminous beam.

(Are there not butterflies for these surf-flowers?
Do not tell me that one ever drowned.
Lingering too long by the gust of some fountain,
Or that those twinkling in teams, parting and closing
The light-dotted vanes of their wings
Ever capsized, riding over a stream
The way song soaring rides down a wind.)

Fountains, our volatile kin,
Coursing as courses the blood,
For we are more water than earth
And less of flesh than a flame
Bedded in air and run by the wind—
Bequeath me, be with me, endow my hunger

With sweet animal nature,
Knit me in with the plumes and the wands of your favor,
Get me great vistas, jade-milky streams
Where the source of the fury starts,
Winking up the last supper of light.
Get me chrysanthemums, great bulky heads,
And a stem narrow as mercury
Fit to support a bluet.
And out of the reflections of water on stone
Let me count the great arcs,
The clusters rounded as grapes
Or staccato as needles,
All that momentum kept firm
Propelled by the dry force of form—
To rest, momentarily at least
In the cataract of time—
Leaves for his feathers on the breast of an eagle,
Deep light of the long nights and years!

III

In this tranquil life such as belongs to windmills
Though the subtle day does not blow
But stands tranced in the wickets
And aspirations of water,
Descend by these paths, these perspectives,
This cascade of steps by the balustrades
Downgliding as if molded out of waves,
Into the white strata and springs
Of the founding place and wedding of waters.
But you must thrice interpret to know,

Mad on the waters, what they vow. . . .
Listen. The fine battery of them.
Like a purification of sound
Blows their deep chanting,
That murmurous persisting.
No wilier song from the moon
Ever plunged into and took apart,
Dividing the plangent strands of it,
Such a fine cornucopia of bloom.

Like a low meditation on song
Before that song has begun,
This speech over you in a mesh,
This chain-mail of running light and of breath,
This tissue as if of sleep
That is so lightly woven
The dream stares through with its Bacchic locks
Till you wear the very cloth of dream at last
Of figured and intertwined emblems.
Walks in long arches under it,
Portals through which if you go
You are into the white-woven web held fast.
But you must thrice interpret to tell
What is said by a flower in a spell,
Ascending the steps to the gods . . .
You may see them among the flowers,
Standing small-headed, vast-eyed,
The grace of the broad breast turned,
A beardful of weeds and small ones
Lurked there by the marble-veined sides.

And you have gone the ways of each sense
To dam up thirst or to stanch it.
There was a wild stream lashed to a tree
Gave out its oracular oratory.
By a flume came thrasonical volley
Boasting of love and struggle.
Through watery walls blown asunder,
So light the small threads of structure,
By so many gadding ways of the senses
Harnessed to water, knowing what fire
Must make their divine toil turn wheels
For the relentless mills and wills
You came from the watery furnaces,
From springs sealed of the sleep
Smoldering with what divinations
If such may arise and wake.

And meanwhile they stand there, they linger,
They recline, they preside, in languor or rigors,
Gods, our great friends of love and rage.
Passion stares into their empty eyes
Want sees the calm sweet water coursing,
Artfully held in their mouths and pulsing,
Blind waters tranquilly stemming there.

A Fable of Berries

(For Cornelius A. Yaple and
Mrs. Margaret Meeker)

The mountain goes straight up behind that house
And the wild apple boughs still hold a ladder in them.
A birdnest in a pan sits on the window sill
And the white spring is piped though it runs free
Down rocks as well.
Springs the wild mountain on every side hard up
Softened and laden down with trees in fissures caught
And the mist, like treks of cloud, spumes past,
Ladders of sight against the shagged green sides
As the handsome girl comes out to drive two cows
To pasture where the salt lick stands.

The wheel in the stream and the tool shed
That was going to be moved, and the worm-holed roof
With its roof-nailed ladder and curlycue shingles
And the high-bent house amazed on its perch
Like a nailed-up birdcage staggered in wind
And the brown river visible, and across up the sides
Like a square in the rocks and bushes, a meadow
Where cows deep in its tassels browse
To mark the already marked ascent—
There the wild gourd grows and one must climb up
To a pitch and an elevation all is so tangled,
Grows without reason, disdains the excuse!
And apples, green, immature, fallen to ground,
And snow balls, white against porous bells of the cloud,
While beyond an uprooted railroad bed
Is a very alley leading, enclosed by trees,
To the spectacular flood of a mountain.

II

It is this that happens in the wind-wrapt morning
When the berries are ripe near Margaretville.
We have come out with wicker and crates
And our quick fingers stained by the sun.
Life is a freshness that milk-mothers know
Bent over cribs to the dark-eyed owl.
Sleep is a cask keeping profundities cool
Though resistance is hooped by steel,
And the cows are let in to pasture out of the moment
The girl comes back from sleepy-licked bolsters.

We were here for the night like peddlers or gypsies.
The old man has settled to fire the chimney
Of the lone old woman who's taken us in;
She has doffed us a welcome and pumped the harmonium
And the two sang together like gay-cheeked birds.
Hotcakes and fritters; the spun house settles
Into its spirits and groans with its winds
In the low-eaved bins where I paced and I slept.
Hung the beams with spiders.
I clothed all their work with demented covers
Dead with love, mad like a horse on apples.
All night whined the shutters, banged looms
Of footbridge clapping and spectral flying
By the slat bed, in the cupboard room
Sprung by the winds, where I wove ropes
The footwork of riggings, interloped seizures
On the sails of love-crazy loons.

While half through the night the thin sounds broke
Of the lily horn from the dust of its corner
That played the thin water of sound,
Played Harry Lauder and turkey-trot bands
Till the lame-legged ones tried a few turns
And of the old times drank a deep chord
And were revived in the salt-rough waters
Where the soul breaks away with a touch or a thread
So delicate rash is the body sprung—
And half through the night the thin sounds broke
Of the lily horn and their clacking talk
Till the bird saying *day* stood on a stalk
The cows went out and a chipmunk ate
Melon seeds while we dippered warm milk
And were off to the berry-laden mountains.
What were we to do with the berries we got?
The old woodchuck of the party questioned not.
The berries were there and they must be picked.
And into the back country with baskets and crates
Filling jugs with water from springs that he swore
Had the whole liquor of dews from rocks
In a car put together with strings we went.

It was in the grape-valley country of peaches, and moles
Small on long spurs full of doors, and ponds
Of green rushes the muskrats delved
And the black-necked goose with its trailing young.
Heights, fulcrums for clouds, and the chipping birds,
Water bushes and long-bladed fields.

III

Much like a long time ago goes this world.
Birds fight in the bush; what is it they say?
Time has strange glasses; take them up.
Seven long years the berries are ripe
And many have married, buried, burned who would eat
Of the dark juice and go mad on it.

The old man is dead, selling bushels and bales
Who had planted a countryside full of elms
And poplars and cedars on occasional days.
And the old lady whirled in her chair
With a glee triumphant because it was cracked—
Twice had the lightning played and her hair crinked—
Do they sing from her bones like a daft cat?
In the habitation of each houseghost
It must be certain some do, I think.
For never we got to the mountains that time
And never the berries he bragged
And the wild ladders of foam fell away before
I could get down from them.
How may I think such a time was?
Clouds stream over, all is half seen.

IV

I shall climb up over the other side
By the back of the way we did not know,
Shall climb up, yes, by the new strange track
Up stinted trees the opposite rock
And arise and find them there,

Find neither myself nor they have gone
Though the field has changed from green to brown.

And surprise them there in the glasses I find
By looking thus in the madness of time
And we shall be rocked in the freshets we knew
Though we have fled from the heavens there were
When, like the sensuality of a new rough star
One came, and was revolution.

Shall climb up, yes, by the other side
Though we did not get to the berries that time.
Do I doubt of the berries that the brambles hid?
In this perspective, whatever sense touches
In the form of things will be seen.
The berries in the brambles shall be found,
We shall even be among mountains then,
In perturbation I will taste again,
And will not come down.

Incantatory Poem

Hearing that you would come who by my love
Have dreamed me into your head these lost long days
I have caught birds and freed their essential blaze
For still I am as always my heart's hungering slave
And thus but dream life into its beat form
Singing up voices out of the wine-gay blood.

Water and wine being the elements
I was big with cliffs and water-wracking rocks
And huger than I my heart hearing your own
Racing thus to come nearest home with cloud
Under its rain-bearing leaves that were your name
Meaning waif of the tribe of cloud and rain,
Hearing that you would come, blood climbed on bone.

Hearing that you would come in the green cold days
Neither good nor great, my wine-flown blood
Got up incanting sleep's towers to the moon
To pray she bring her sailing presence round
From the back of night that she flag you home
(And dry brook beds she rushes into sound)
Lest all be storm-blown out to deeps
Raging beyond your name, and you not come
By spring's first fields already clad
To herald your long ride down.

By spring's first fields where the darkness there
Rose up to put your wild warmth on
Till absence shaped your body by absence learned
On the pitch of dark to light at my very hand

Under whose pulse you lay where my shaking heart
By its long stroke got you out of sleep
Into dream's childing origins.
Your name wearing water in cloud and flame
The world bearing flowers out of your name
Or in the dim sleep nothing borne
But the sound of waters racing your blood
And the running of waters and the dim
Bemused confession of waters foretelling your coming,

Bearing in morning over the threshold
South-infused, storm-centered, surly,
Purely peace-seeking as the rose
Till wonder lay waking at the heart early
Hearing that you would come for whom by my love
Bells and their tongues wait,
Birds in the bell of the bush their small songs halt.

Hearing that you would come
By the waters charged with your traveling home
On the speed of the surf-worked spume,
I make a prayer I shape upon a poem
Cut from the essential dealers of the green,
Too long dissembled from the water-swearing birds
And make a poem I shape upon a prayer
To this all-fathering dark now come to flower
When day has broken and we lie
Crossed with birds out of your name
I stole by watches of the griefless dream
In the element of the wine-transfiguring world.

My Frantic Heart

My frantic heart awoke
In the middle of the night.
What foot trod the stairs?
Who sobbed below in the street?
The crawling silence told
Nothing, and my loud heart shrieked.

The image of the sufferer
Abides at every street.
These mourning crowds at noon
Numb to their exit, break
For entrance that has no retreat.
The concrete and the buildings sink
Imagination to a terrible use.
Our passion wastes against a vile produce.

Such darkness falls from day
How may you and I and they
Endure enschooled reality?
No taxi stops to let you out
No foot is running on the stair
And all forgiven, all forgot,
That makes you and redemption what
Frees a whole society
From the death that it knows not.

Their living death is in my heart.

And you, my only one, who've gone
And return not, nor will,
The image of your stricken face is they
And I am crying in the street miles away.

The Land We Did Not Know

With what fond ignorance we came
To all that land that did not know we were
Which cared not if we lay upon its downs
And took our worship for the thing it had
From all eyes passing by that way.
It takes more ignorance than the heart can say
To stare as we did at each tree and stone
As if we'd found a world unknown
When gravestone upon gravestone in the wood
Has lost its names and half its words
In the dark avalanche of snows and dews
And all the rains and pickings of the birds.

It takes such passion as the ignorant know
Who out to save that folly, tell the dead,
Tell books and history, ignorance is delight—
As if it were! And yet to keep pitch pure
Must hope to know the thing unknown
As if both they and it had just begun—
Which only can be reached to through those eyes
And hungered lips that measured out the scope
And gave to each bird kin and each stone name
In the felicitous unity all would make.

The passion is to keep the ignorance
Till wonder gets so saturate with the thing not known
You have become the thing you knew by loving most
What most compels us to the land's beginning.
And thus, my upland slope, I touch you here
Incredulously, like one who comes
To greet you, walking on the tiptops of the trees.

FROM

Country Without Maps

1964

Cortège for Colette
(THE PALAIS-ROYAL GARDENS)

Minister of birds,
Keeper of islands and pools
Where they sink and go down in races
By the mosses and deep scattered sedges,
Collector of grasses, seed-heavy and bent,
Seed of the fern and the violet,
(Known to the moonmen and the green fever),
All receipts and brews, felicitous cures
Under sinewy roofs and streets of the root.

Genius, moreover, of gardens,
The bowknot, the crescent, and square,
And as many circular knots, and that pruning art
The shears do so well with the snail,
Tender and trainer of fountains,
Benefactor of boxwood, quincunx, and yew,
Mathematician of the parterres
By a lapful of sparrows,

I have heard, I have come by these arches and urns,
All the classical battery of forms
Through the rectangular perspectives
Down the long galleries that end in the windows.
Closed are the gates. The calm is great
In the dark, where the small waters blow.
There is a sense of a slow sailing out
As a sudden wind tries a few leaves.
A part of a cloud interrupts the passage
Of the knobbed moon.

And I do not think the garden is what it was.
Like a promise departed, the rectangular perspectives
Down the long galleries end in the windows,
Stop with the shutters.
Should I speak I would not be heard
There where the moon slowly sails on,
For where might there be another speech
Such as signs give, and omens,
Such as sense has in those dreams
For which there is no translation except
In the absolutely unheard music about, perhaps, to be given,
Like a part of the secret sky broken off
Just at the surface where it crowds
With those vaguely summoned to take the long turns of the dance?

But let me not, standing outside these gardens,
These oblong gardens, this file of trees
Subject in dark to a murmur of days
Held echoing under their leaves,
Where only some sliver of water sighs,
Spilling over and over into its pool,
Where under the yellow light of the lamps
Only a cat walks, it is late for the arcades
Out of the gardens to keep their own life,
And for low doors opening into mossed courts,
Let me not, to the diminished perspectives
Hovered with ivy where an urn sits, declare
That a part of the world having gone back into itself,
A meaning is thereby lost,
The disappearance of which torments us,
For it was not subtle but gross.

Amidst all this matching of flowers and shapes,
This tending of borders, this cutting by trowels,
Though compelled to pay close attention and not to walk blindly
As if in a massacre of petals,

To know
That that of which you were the great witness lives,
That the torn butterfly will not leave the page,
Pierced by the light you gave,
That by the power not to forget
Profoundly connecting with the root
You brought by its weight some perfected whole
Of a part of the self into flower,
Who lightly go to the grave,
Having expended all you could give.

Nor to speak of the corruption of ivy
Nor of absence where presence dwells
Nor of darkness where there is love.
To be mute, to be mute about death,
To address the invisibles
For whom your genius, like a delicate beast
Training your heart,
To your sense giving lessons,
Led you out of the one world
Into how many nuages—embarkings!

And simply to lift up the flower,
Simply to salute the cloud,
From the cat to the horse by way of the dragon,
To some striped sky by way of the bird

That it be borne, your body,
In the arms of young men round and round
And to the march blown by bugles
That the dark iron of its velvet vow
Shock through the blood some understanding
Just as sensory as perfume when the touched body
Gives forth the divine humors of rain and leaves.

Of a Day and Hares

Dürer's brown hares were in a cage
With their long soft ears laid flat,
Their oblong eyes closed, in some feigned sleep,
Only their whiskers alive
In the perpetual tremor of very fine things.
A guinea pig to each hare slept on each hare's back.
It was, for September, a hot day
And there was that fur close to fur and warming it.

We have lost much time by love affairs,
By a pedantic madness we have lost the rest.
Animals have time. We lose it.
When we lose we are lost. We are marking time with the days
We are letting them die away.
In retrospect we see the dwindling host,
We are fierce judges of what cost us tears most.
To judge ourselves is as to see ourselves
Grandiose in plight. We see ourselves and think that we may laugh.
Salubrious is laughter. Or a short barking unhappy and ugly.
If we would not lose time, what would we be?
That which no doubt we are.
But does it alter? Perhaps.
If between being and doing there were not a gulf.
The animals for whom we have too much respect of a sentimental variety
Supposedly dwell in the mindless flow. Is being mindless purity?
Does it partake of an indefinable grace?
We lie down in the grass and hear time moving over us.
Its bells that flay the air flay us.
Or in the light rumble of its wheels the weight is going over us.

Or then to stroll . . .
Alone before God or nothingness . . .
For the guinea pigs and the hares will be sold
Or caged. Only the air we cannot use
Or hurt is free. Only the air and light we cannot cage
That play upon this day so soundlessly. . . .

Amsterdam Letter

Brick distinguishes this country,
And broad windows—rather, rectangles
Of wide and glittering scope—
And cabbages.
Cattle a specialty, and cheese, storks—if they are not all dead
Or abandoned—and flowers, oh, flowers!
Some say as well, quick humor.
Is it a specimen of humor that a cabdriver proposes to marry me?
The speaking of English is at least general.
Also I have spoken a little Dutch with an old Frisian lady.
How affable she was, amusing and helpful!
(They *are* helpful and affable, and their far too occasional teams of horses
Wear rosettes by the ears.)
Aside from that, and above all, the dense, heavy, fragrant sky
And rich water, a further extension of color—
The sky a low window over this twining of green water and bridges—
And the sedate, gabled houses pressed closely together
And bicyclists, six abreast or more,
Skimming round corners like swallows.
How quiet they are! even the trolleys!
While the trains seem to glide like sleighs on runners
So that after those many places dedicated, it would seem, to clatter
The absence of it becomes an active delight in itself.

The delight is in part, of course, the lovely dividing of the city
By those ancient and ripe-green canals, and the mixed fragrance
Of the River Amstel and roasting coffee,
And the bravura of carved animal heads, the elegance of panels,
And those panes of violet and panes flushed yellow
That alternate the clear meaning of glass

With the blindness of shutters closed over warehouse windows,
And that Gothic German French sense of the arabesque and the scroll,
The urn and the garland of leaves.

As for that delicacy of manner, that responsiveness to many,
That prevalence of what seems self-possessed, contained, and easy—
I am speaking of those who went out of their way
To lead me to Rembrandt's house
(Which in his lifetime he lost),
Of the woman at the Cantine,
Of the Madame, too, in the Zeedjik,
Amiable conversationalists
Who did not make me feel stupid
Because I would never speak their language,
Who by a manner suggested
What I have no word for—
Unfeigned it is and unblighted,
That "generous, free disposition"
That so strongly confirms
A fitness of things,
As do also the upright geraniums,
All of which, by the elm-dark canals
(Where dogs on the loose loped up to me
With cold, wet noses
And ducks paddled under the Seven Arches
And the gilt swan rode on the crest of the fortified tower),
Offered some measurable glimpse of what
There, by the water beds
And the ancient, calmed passions of their reflections,
Informed me as the moon does,

Which was in part the pleasure of learning
Those words that I did from the old Frisian woman—
Horse, sky, cow, tree, thank you, I mean,
Beauty, and love.

Invitation to a Hay

A settlement of love
Is what I'd risk if you would.
A central fountain and a horse,
A little native elegance,
Some green-shuttered saffron buildings
And avenues of leaning trees
And an orchard close by
Divided from a field of hay
By a mouldering old wall
Snaking up a hill.
I'd have a garden primed
With beanflowers and chick peas
And in tubs lemon trees
Not to forget the marveled orange—
Where is a fruit so bright
And a stem so delicate?—
And days of blue air
That crowd the dark boughs of a grove
And other days as pale
As light in a birch grove—
Oh birch my very white
And original delight!
And back of us and all around
For the castle-haunting rooks
To fly to and fro from
The many-sided, dark-blue faced
Mountains, wrinkled, ravined, cleft
When they are not cast upon
By those pallors that beyond
Tell of a snowlight's origin.

And in this civil order
Ringed round by a wilderness
I'd have some very conical
And shaggy house of hay
To invite you in to stay
As long as butter-yellow walls pleased you
And there you'd be with me
We'd live in a monument of hay
Mad as those who know
In love is all fantasy.
Your breast would be of burning gold
And its delicious heat
Would warm me day and night
While creatures of the wood
Might envy, if they could,
Our joy just as fine
As the improvising clouds
That as you look at them are gone
Or volatile as leaves in wind.
We'd go bird-nesting in clouds
And hunting down the meadow grass
For flowers or the smallest haunts
Of the young field mice.
And in this ancient landscape
Preponderant with moss,
Rambling walls and pinewoods
Of narrow alleys at the end of which
Daylight stares starkly through,
Our love alone would be new
Despite its ancient properties.

Aërial would we be
With love's finest courtesies,
By all that shapes of earth and air
Can subtilize the senses with
Until they have grown rapt
On emanations of a light
When fold on fold goes into
Five fathoms of a blue.
Our love would be endowed
By mountain and by cloud
So long as we would stay
Alongside such ravines
And such slopes of terraced vines
Broken towers and bells
In a shaggy house of hay.
My dear, and will you be
Content to dwell with me
Eating of illusion
Daily and nightly?

"Thy Love Is One Thou'st Not Yet Known"

Let us be quiet today. The earth is still,
The sun is drowsy, sleeping in the clouds
Like sleepless birds of day who take to rest
Or take at least to silence in their nests
Only some very few adventured out
To stride the levels of the rusty grass.

But for the crickets in a singsong shrill
Of notes too small to be called notes,
Some tick and jilt of quaver in the low tangle
Soprano as some fifing of an elf
Or other hopping creatures made of green,
Green-whiskered, green-antennaed, green-armored,
There is no other cry or breath.
                              Air is still
As every flower tells and every leaf,
And waters where they were subside to wells
Or sink their resourceful chatter underground.

As if the quick of all that stir and bloom
By brook and wind commotion, ceaseless play
Of clouds, leaves, action of the plants
That in their beds stand taller every day
Had taken a quietus or, quiescent,
Retired into some first most voiceless place
Begot by silence on a stillness,
An in-going into the unlustred zone
Of some more hermit energy
That gets the tendrils of the sense
Their dwelling place in a white hush

And makes the instant finer than a dream.
But is not dream but rather's known
By burning fineness of a light
More lucid than the air and only sensed
In violent wide-awakeness on a cloud.
Only by the raveling of such bonds
As strips the day to garments of the flower—
To leaning lilies much too tall
To sustain their flaring crowns,
Veronica, vervain, bent over by the rain,
And Queen Anne's lace upon its gawky stem.

Her Spring Song

If I could live once more to see those flowers,
The daffodils and the bloodroot,
Those white, frail, long-petaled stars,
And a gang of crocuses,
Said the old woman with a clump
Of rosebushes she would plant,
Her hands thorn-pricked and scratched.

And hear that bird of sharp sweet song
Nor be deaf to its low cry
Nor blind to the flowers, I mean, both see
And hear the way I did when I
Danced as I walked
And had no need of any prop

And would do so now but that
Another wind blows
And I ache with the water over the stones
And where the wind tumbles the weirs
And the trouble of leaves scudded by airs
And ache with what each day
Must roll the sun around.

And have I lived too long
To keep enchanted eyes? And who was it said
That we improve with the years?
And yet to live without
The sense of the pulse of things,
No longer to keep time
To that pure animal tune,

To live without that. Not even a beast
Has to live so. And the work with the leaves,
The work with the earth,
The work, preparing for flowers,
To live, not knowing if
Because of what I do they'll thrive,
To have not even the imperative
Of sensitive plants that close
When light thins out and goes,

Impenitent upon my knees,
Hurt by the thing I love,
Not to pray to be possessed
Down under even death
By things as they were
When in their substance, firm and clear,
I thought I knew what all lived for,

And unwarily, unwarily,
Took so much to heart
It pulled the strings apart.

Epitaph for My Cat

And now my pampered beast
Who hated to be wet,
The rain falls all night
And you are under it.
Who liked to be warm,
Are cold as any stone,
Who kept so clean and neat,
Cast down in the dirt
Of death's filthy sport.

Proem

Now waiting in difficult rooms of justice
For the assent that will not come, insurrecting theorem
On which could have been based the dissident structure of happiness

And waiting in the brown dispassionate autumn
Grimacing with rain as leaves are mashed
By the hard errands of the anonymous foot

Under the monotonous sky that governs plains
And ruins, declensions of the past's soiled promissory,
Counting the time until the full hour blows

Among the leaves and fall of hours
When voices rash with envy, retribution
Mouth once again the well-bred lies

Of neat and heavy houses where
Regularity would stifle difference, rebellion
Is an adolescent vice, typical of the spoiled, ungifted derelict:

I would search out the subject that will not decay
Willing that by such patience I will not lose patience
Despite the inchworm crawl of this destructive time,

Crude refuse, backwash of the late disfigured past,
Nor bay against the dogs of dissolution.
So if crude action tells again my deaths

And wounds are quicked to life, the gape begins
Impossible to stanch, a kind of inorganic struggle of the blood,
Yet by resolve build resource, set

Faith at insult, love against the crazed impulse
To hate, and so find calm in terror.
The wet leaves molder, pale, and turn to meal

And waiting's less a test of revelation
Than test to see how quietly I turn
And cur-like snarl at what I'd once cherished

When back like scavengers my gifts return
Loathed, now loathsome, that were once so hearty.
And thus, like one before the dead

Paused so and huddled like a thick bundle,
To stand against these broken meanings that would paralyze
And sting to death the separate parts of consciousness

Or conscience, in an inactive hell.
And wait: as if a continuity
Inheres, outweighs, like roots, this passageway of leaves

So harshly driven to yield up their place:
Knowing full well how once again such waiting may be dupe,
Fiasco occasioned by the overt lack,

Arraigned as well by gorged and slippery luck.
More useless than a broken arm the gun
Or all defense against the terrible one,

Or all offense, old leader love,
Dead angel we deceive. . . .

New York: Summertime

1

Those rumors and orchestras
Of the playgrounds of summer—
Children!
Parked trucks of the ovaled cheeks
And sleek skin of the cut watermelon!
Bells of the traveling parlors
And snow-wagons of ice cream!

Your pale stifling room
Glazed by the porcelain light
Of pulled Venetian slats.
Half-naked now we sit
Our arms so bare we seem to touch
Though we don't do so
And so much else exposed
Through your walkup's open doors—
The hairy husband in his underwear,
The sweating housewife slumped
On a kitchen chair,
Van Gogh prints and mottoes on the walls—
"Here is the time to live and why not now!"

In your room's glazed pallor
The oven's burning toast.
Your many mirrors garble
Parts of light and float.
Touch is burning up the toast,
The mirrors scorch that hold
Our drowned-in-shadow faces in them.

Boop of the saxaphone
Those sugar'd waltzes slurping.
It is! I am! I am! screams
Summer in a heat.
It is! You are! You are!
My stupored blood beats back.

And you, child of the violent season,
Who buy your playtime in the bars,
Who'd blaze away the moment like they do
Upon their hopscotch squares
Or by some streetlamp shrilling late
With cards and fires—
They tell me how your nature's blent
With what's so shaped and colored still
By this half-cracked omphalos of
The fevers of our screwed-up fate—
Crazes of the dynamo!

Your restless energy that thirsts!
Your forced elations that like rockets burst
Their salvos upon nothingness!
A spendthrift tempest that I hear
Your hammering heart beat out
To the convulsive pulse
Our motored generations make!

2
And you, child of the violent season,
The summer's kissing you.

A *blague*. It's I who kiss
It's I who strive in blood
To get this mixing done
Of motored air that whines
With the continuous burr
Of exiled insects dead.
Some desiccated grief-in-fear
Now in the populous midst
Of energies that strain
With passion at the leash
Because it is the time to live!
Because exploding chemistries
Tell us so and tell
Of the hurled-at star. (We hear
The howling dog in space.)
Our fate like his is brief and short,
Succinct as melting summer on the limbs
Though in the senseless go
Of bodies to get wet and faint
We may feel less isolate.

Now, put up in quietude,
Freed of that frenzied churn,
It's you and you and you who still beat on
To make the wild percussion in my mind
Though it's the mourning dove that moans
And deafening crickets grind
Against those pastimes of the horn
The sizzling locusts wind
And tattered hollyhocks decline.

That bounding ball, the radios
That played around your court,
Your frittered pulse that leapt
With the stertorous breath
That twists an impulse into flame—
Of these I make my monody:
To action that pretends it knows,
To necessity that says
It was before we chose
That which we're burning in,
To our splendor and our waste.

A Note to La Fontaine

I have come into the time of the ant.
The grasshoppers are bitterly paying.
Their fiddles are broken, they are lame and laid up,
The ants are sneering: "Now dance!"
And the grasshoppers, in an ague of shivering,
Faint for a morsel, seem to be trying.
It is not good to see. How may I have this tribe starve?
It is a slap in the face of all I believe
To concede that the sour ones, safe in their barracks
Where they so promiscuously scurry,
Should have every right to be dry and ironic.
Survival is *not* the test, and is a long life the best?
Fie on the righteous dullards
So proud of their sweltering summer labor
That allows them to live without honor through winter.
The grasshoppers have more grace
Than to make out for themselves any case.
With that knowledge they'll die
Spitting into the bleak eye
Of those who never had such song
To make life seem dancing and warm.

Upon the Intimations of Love's Mortality

It is the effort of the lie
Exacts a wounding pulse.
I loved you much
When everything had excellence at once.
First was our freshness and the stun of that.
Your body raved with music. What was lost
Is just that element our time always takes
And always in love we venture off some height
The nothing else can equal after it.
The thought of that bedevils me for miles.
How can I save you from my own despair
To think I may not love you as before?
Spoiled, we become accustomed to our luck.
This is the devil of the heart.
We were the smiles of gods awhile
And now, it seems, our ghosts must eat us up
Or wail in temples till our tombs are bought.
Attended now by shades of that great while,
Disguise is the nature of my guile
And yet the lie benumbs the soul.
Get me the purity of first sight!
Or strength to bear the after light.

Pays Perdu

There are those days, vivid and pure,
When everything dazzles, new found.
It is on days like this that we understand Eden,
Old worlds of the Golden Hours.
What is it. It is vigor, freshness,
A sense of the flags of day flying free,
It is commodious harmony,
We have fallen into some deepest relation
With self, the sense, and the world,
We are at rest strenuously
For all has form, moves with vivacious fluidity.
Then—nothing that seems extraneous
From the voices of bells caught, parted and cast away
To the blazings of twenty butterflies
Bemused on a stalk of blue flowers.
As if we had composed the day
With the sleeping unseen at the back of the mind
And we neither faint nor pale.
'When we are happy we have other names.'

So it was on that day in the country
When my friend and I at large in a town
Fortified in its rock above a green river
(A champing and nervous force that had cut
Whole landscapes in two in its glacier course)
Started out at the height of noon
On the broad footpath by the river
Past gardens of garlic and artichoke
And groves of olive established in tiers.
It was in Provence and by the Var

In a country of vineyards and lizards
And the fragrance of many rough herbs in bloom,
St. John's Eve, almost, and yet not come,
The perfect summer essence of the year.
Now, as we were along the way
We stopped to talk to a passerby
Proud to dispense the lore of the country,
A stranger herself, who spoke of a village
Far down the way, by the river, and of another
Far up in the mountains, hard if not impossible to find,
From which donkeys came down twice a week,
There being no road but a donkey track
And this track its only link with the world.
She herself had seen neither one
But she liked to think of them lurking
At the end of some straggling path. So did we,
And following her vague suggestion
That the one called Lacs, up in the mountains,
Was somewhere *down* and then *up*, set out,
Larky and confident.

This much we knew, that in an old country
That holds many bones, where life has been hard,
Where much dust of the nightingale
Is mixed with the dust of poppies
And the stubborn roots of valerian, and all
The medicinal sages,
That in an old country crossed by centuries of animals and men
There are many paths possible to take.
Foxes and dogs made them first,
Horses and donkeys succeeded.

Then the paths were secured, steps were cut out,
Walls were erected.
An old country is criss-crossed with paths,
Short cuts to the crest of a mountain.
Look at some track up the terraces
Where the olive trees doze
And you ought to know it is going somewhere.
We took one on some such faith.

  II
And of the three-hour walk in the blaze of day
Up the snail-spiralling way of the rough country—
Scrub-oak and stone—
And the three vertigoes when the path fell sheer
By the cliffside straight to the river
And there was white limestone dust and a chalky glare
Blinding—
    and the heat—till we cooked—
And knew the beginnings of thirst—
       and were lost

Or deceived by a choice of paths
So retraced our steps to a farm
And the goat-faced owner who had been asleep
Shouting down from the upper story window
(After his dogs had barked themselves hoarse)
That if we wanted to visit a *pays perdu*
Take the fork back there to the left—

And of the way up by hawk's beak and claw
By rock horn and fang and skull,
By the death's head grin of the spurred headlands

As the path twisted inland
Broad enough at times for two donkeys
But losing us in the basil and marjolain
And long ceased the groves of the flickering olive,
The derelict houses and storing sheds
As we climbed on past a pine wood,
The sun glinting on their tufts and their cones
And baking the rock formations.
And into what were we going, leaving the river,
That broad boulevard, that viable thread,
To go back and into the crowded interior,
Crowded, that is, with trees and more rock and many small mountains
That engendered, for all that we knew, cockatrices. . . .
And at one turning in a medley of rubble
Meeting a child, a little girl,
Carrying a basket that had a cloth cover
Who was so startled on seeing us and hearing us speak
That we thought her a mute, she taking so long to answer
And then in a voice as if rusty from long disuse.

This was the first stage; after that, more declivities,
More mournful ostentation of stone as we climbed
And knew thirst and passed through more deadlands
Meeting the sense of the torture of time.
History is time and it assailed us, the sight of those signs of that static
    tempest that had once pressed forth those needles of rock that once
    again met us, and the swirled water-marked rippled bad-rock effects
    across yet another harsh breach in earth's crust cut by the Var's
    tributary

And if music is the energy of time, immensely loading some quarter-
    hour with the compressed violence of meanings too numerous, shades

too elusive striving against the iron gates and in one crazed hurl
achieving the leap, so the ever continuing variations of new fantasies
of rock made us laggard. Impressed us? Oppressed us.
Ejaculations of rock pipes with crumbling flutings! Perches for birds or
stylites, grotesque and badly botched Byzantine pillars!

And our weak shoes half in ribbons from so much pulverizing by pebbles.
And we streaked with sweat and the taste of much dryness in the mouth.
Grown over by land, by what we had seen,
Bruised by the stones white with dust and pollen,
Burnt by the sun in a mirth
Of the incurable singing of the nightingale.
For we had spied on the bird in a round bush
Though that was below, near the river.
Up here, in the miles inward, bees followed us
But not that Greek thrush. Here it was birdless,
Wildness in waste,
And the disintegrating black schist,
Porphyry headlands, beetling and angled . . .

And then, by a turn, roofs!
And our drouth drank of the cordial.
For here would be the douce water, casks of it, vats,
And we dreamed up the *café*, for what town was without one,
Where we would sit, steeped in mineral water,
Citron pressé, and after that *café*
Before we'd begin on water again.

But as a mountain is never the same
When you are traveling toward it,
Presenting at each turn another view of its one hundred faces

And as space itself is as deceiving,
So we lost that prospect, another turning swallowed it up,
We jogged on, thinking of donkeys
And what sort of people were these who lived so far inland?
And who could ever take over these mountains?
Dense earth resisted, hail to its lordship
That would thrust us out of its holdings!

Nor by more turnings did the roofs swim back
Although we came to a bridge
Where the path broadened into a road.
Now the sky was staring with a sudden stark blue
Over the flank of a new mountain
And two or three paths coiled before us.
All was less wild, we had modulated
Into what might have been at one time subdued
By the plough, though forgotten by now,
A table of land half pasture,
And we went this way and that
Attempting to skirt the shape of the land.
Was it a mirage? We half joked.
Had our thirst started up a fever so soon?
Wasn't it an hour ago we had seen
The tiptilting roofs? Into what had they gone?

Then suddenly a wheatfield
And a lane or a gulley of stones and a sharp hill
Up which we stumbled into storm blue,
The sky full of violent, crazed blue,
And a wind rolling in the trees

By a haycock shaped like a loaf of bread
And truly the roofs and surely the water!
And we running now across the shorn field
Till we came to the first faces of houses.
The field rode up to their windows
And the shutters on them were closed
And the silence could not be more unstirred
Until we called out and black and white doves
Started up with a creak of wings
And we called again. But where were the people?
Was it inhabited by black and white doves or pigeons?

And we went around a corner, if you can call it that, between one house
    with its roof fallen in and one whole one and came into a courtyard
    with lime trees in bloom and three or four houses across the way and
    saw a woman wearing a man's peaked hat and a man's shoes running
    with a pack of hay on her back and a woman in a big straw hat and
    three dogs that came at us snarling and as the wind buffeted the lime
    trees and the crazed blue grew stalwart we saw *this* was the town but
    there was the water running from a pipe's mouth into a tub. What
    a stir! for if we were apparitions to them they were not less to us, and
    the dogs barking for all they were worth till a man called them off
    and one who had been willing to hurl himself at our throats now
    wagging his tail as we explained how long we had been walking and
    —THIRST! And he pointed triumphantly to what they had
    an abundance of.

Then we rather crazy there at the tub, filling our hands with water.
And my friend lying prone and drinking from the pipe's mouth . . .
While bundles of hay kept flying past us on the backs of the man and
    woman and the one in a straw hat calling out to them in a language

we had never heard to which was added the delirium of birds just
before rain—swallows springing out of nowhere to shriek and to skirl
and a swooping by pigeons while a battery of crows cawed by.

And as the storm sky humped down I running out in the unearthly blue
to the 'other side' of the town . . . which was likewise a field that
stretched off to a mountain. But more. Much more. Where I stood
was before the very birth of a chaos of definable forms.
So here they were, put down in a lull, the last lull between peaks.
Since to the 'back' or the 'north' stretched that beginning of the one
thousand wrinkled circus-tent tops.

Till the rain came down in a blithe bluster of spears and the air was so
freshened with the breath of all that seems good that the rain froze
and we were peppered with a fine shot of hail and took refuge under
a shed until the man who had been carrying hay asked us into his
house.

And we saw, going in, a bright blue postbox at the side of his door.

And we went into the first black room
Filled with blossoms of the lime tree in gunny sacks
And loose on the floor and on a table, and into the kitchen
With an iron stove and scraps in a pan on the floor for a dog
And the woman in the peaked hat was there
With eyes that ate up her face
Nodding to us and smiling but sitting away where we could not see her,
Sitting away in a corner like a bird mewed up,
And her husband eager to do the talking
With the stub of a burnt-out cigarette
In the corner of his mouth like a sore,

Slight and not young,
His beret jammed tight to his head . . .
And he wanted to know just how we had happened to come
Because, where they were, few did
And was it true that the donkeys went down
Twice a week or more? we asked.
About that, he was vague. Yes, he had donkeys
And when the wheat was cut—
We understood then that truly at times
The donkeys went down with produce
And returned with provisions.
And we heard of the postman who came twice a week
Five miles by the ravines and the gorges
Because there was a postbox and it was the law
Whether there was mail or not—
And of a teacher who also came
Twice a week or so for the one child left.
So. They were not forgotten. He voted.
And they had gone to war,
Two families left now, and one child.
And Lacs had been named for a lake
That had disappeared so long ago
Not even his father's grandfather had seen it
And this house—almost as old!
They had had sheep till the shepherd had left
And years ago there had been hundreds—
Sheep, that is, with their shepherds
Up from the valley to stay the whole summer.
In his father's day there had been horse roads
Now grown over, and the houses for lizards. . . .

He was quick and gentle in the way he spoke
Wearing a cigarette that would not stay lit,
Steadfastly refusing our own.
No animal earth-spirit, weathered and contrary,
But equable, civil,
We felt that it pleased him to talk,
Especially of the heroical postman,
And the thistle hearts that his mother cooked
For the good that it did them;
Like that herb that she swore if you put in your shoe
You could walk miles and never get tired
But he used to walk to the valley half the nights of the week.
Youth was his herb.

And of what else we talked about . . .
As the lime blossoms trembled in the next room
Where a wild bee stumbled and throbbed. . . .
Of the grass fire that made the bees leave
(When they kept bees) and bees won't come back
To a place that's burned
And the mushrooms and snails that came after rain
And one time, long after midnight,
The chapel bell rang and rang
And whether the wind or an animal rang it,
For the rope had worked loose, they never knew.

And the strange Lacs stirred for us
As the lime blossoms trembled in the next room
When he peopled the sides of hill,
Had carts jolting by that took wheat to a mill,
Humors of barnyards, the Gaulois cock crowing,

For which once we left it, there could be no maps.
Pays perdu! said the goat-faced man
And *lacs* also meant a snare made with strings
To catch birds with, as we understood.

And who was to say that their souls were held
In the space here in between mountains
As the thyme and the rosemary perfume the shadows
That the great bodies cast down from their crowns?
And who was to speak of mountain flowers
That can blossom only after snow and deep frost,
Their colors intensified by the rare air,
Resisting the aridity, the cold nights, the poverty of soil,
Indeed, these very deprivations, that struggle
Being necessary for their perfection of a few days?
It was not to say this
                    in the great light
And the forms aloof over the serenity of ruins.

And we took the long way down,
Loping along it easily in the cool of the day,
Not tormented by thirst,
As the small perfumes of earth began to be freed,
The dry-shod ferny gusts,
And shawls of blue shadow cast
On the pale green of dented slopes
Whole peaks in shadow
And whole landscapes in cloud—
"Those intricate thoughts, those elaborate emotions—"
Where at the converging of four peaks
A cloud makes a fifth.

New Poems

Set forth upon the flowing night
Or what craft was this of flight
By shifting dream before a pane
That seemed to hold the moon-made tent?
I did not know, so caught
Where dream and memory met
For this was one my heart knew well
That now a dark did drink.
Deep the quaff. His struggle wild
Those bands and seals to break
Until it grew my own who saw
That moon-made thing swell out
On silver-coated waters tracked
By skeins and circles of the light
And struggled then to smash the pane
That held the mirror up to dream
Of what was passing that I saw
Had happened and that yet must be
And struggled with an aerial strength
So alien and so intimate
To clarify—like horns by sea
Odd triumphs of a revelry!
There was suspension then
As before the wave descends
Before, flung up and held,
It plunges, broken, glittering
Into the crawl and sucking of the ebb
Until I knew that what I saw
Was the performance of a rite
And this, the rite, all we may do

In the action of the heart,
Thought bodied forth and past
The place where tears start
As those full swollen sails went out
And knew another dreamed my dream
Though those sails had taken him
And sang now to my dream a song
As if were borrowed the sea's slow voice
As if a thousand shells sighed out
What wind has told to them,
Rough tones commanded by a pulse
Hoarse, silken, like the sea's slow breath
Until the pane went dark.

Fierce memory that is
Co-genitor with dream,
Did you speak out to me,
Another thing from another world
Because a light had surged
From out the dark it had gone through
To rise again, like some pronged star,
Or a bough dipped in light,
Glittering like a crystal, what
Dream upon death's heights had met?
An instant then to blaze the pane
Before life's other life begins
That rides the fluent force
And binds the fiery light
That strikes the sunrise coast.

An Improvisation upon the Theme of
The Lady and the Unicorn
(MUSÉE DE CLUNY)

These are her angels!
Frighten us not with seven heads on a stalk!
They guard her sleep in a parable of flowers,
The plumed porcupine
And he of the great horn in the middle of his head
Who paws with laughing modesty the rose standard
Or in a pavilion wears armorial bearings,
Goat-bearded, his breast broader than day,
Breasting the pennant more white than she
Whose skin sheds light as she bathes white in a pool
Where the flutist blows

By a field of blue upon the rose, rose red
And flowers, her simple flowers, degrees of rose,
Where on the dark blue he of the red stocking'd legs proffers
The small heart split at the top that the fingers hold

And flowers, her simple flowers that print the day,
Her Michael-fighting pennant, rose and gray,
And major beasts and lesser beasts, those winged stags
Exultant as deities, whiteness, her rose,
Over which a pennant emblazoned with three moons
More formal and more salient than the sea
Sails out to greet the swollen-bellied ship
That flaunts with answering streamers in the bay

By this, primavera, in the morning of the year
And by daisies, the arbiters of justice and goodness,
Is she appointed to her destiny,

And the red heart burns like a jewel or a fire,
We are held by the heart as he hands it
Not to be played with or eaten by his lady.
The flowers revolve with the beasts around it
While from the knee joints of armor stare faces
And the lion is clasped by his fetlock,
His spanieled feet and arched tongue flared
Like the backwards foil of the lily.

While the unicorn without pasture or fence
Beholds his face stitched in the glass,
Who white as day lights up dark speech,
Maintaining the lion's valor. Though he looks
In a glass at his image, he need not,
He suffers he singular, needing none other,
Though in the herbage you may see him again,
Reduced in stature.
               Need not look in the glass
(Being of the glass, lord of the maze and enigma,
Where each thing to its degree
Is beheld in its entity,
Such as Reynard, such as the dove, and the wolf
Fallen headfirst into a trap, and the porcupine
Plumed, it would seem, or his quills supine),
Who is Quintessential,
Toute Belle,
Pursuivant to all that was hunted for,
Who glides inwoven in flowers, himself the pulled thread,
Infinite relations in his train

In the *perceforest* of shadow.
Who gives a scripture to smiling eyes,
To the small mouth that sweetly psalms,
Being all signs and figurés of love.

Blood and the whiteness of day,
She of the sole desire, dogs, deer,
Stupendous bear embracing,
The hare that leaps against a stretched rope
In the season of venery,
Each with his part in the thirsty quest,
Subjects all of the single objective;
Truly they, like the planets, whirl in an earth order!
Truly here, in a fresh candor,
The bather bathes in the parapets of lilies,
And earth bears everywhere the upstanding flower,
Fruit wood with yellow quince clearly,
Clearly in a fresh candor conceived.
The vair-rose trumpet that her Michael blows,
He jams the dragon to its knees,
And the small heart sparkles amidst the leaves
Of the one thousand flowers, and flares.

Estates of the Loire

It is for as much as we know
Made for the delight of that vassal, the eye,
Richly painted, rimmed like a cat's,
So that the velvet of the green iris
Swims in a fume over fume
Before such lightness and grace
Launching upon its bold course
Of emblems, initials and arabesques,
Panoplied with the heraldic beast,
Sea-silvered in azures, figured in gold,
Till subdued by so much necessity
Of marvel and longing, of trepidation,
It softly closes on some faltering glimpse
Down the green-baized grove,
Hearing every imagining
Of the coming and going of mothed footsteps,
The closing of doors on the lost rooms
Where the insect dryly ticks
Off huge stifling heart-tired strokes;
If before that it is an encounter on fields
When a wind comes to trifle with leaves,
Turrets that flow onto pennons that lavish their tongues
On every chance to stiffen and flare
Before towers so quick to the abutment of towers
There is not room for the pronouncement of more;
A blazoning too beside bridges,
An absorption by flowers subverted in tiers,
That ganged assortment not purely of color;
Intricate double stairways up which they passed
Into the descendant regard of the other;

On the roof a very second city
Tiaraed with the stone royal lily
And ever the effervescence of salamanders
Held in the carved foils of flames
It is less that an understanding is beggared
By these mazes of boxwood bitter in dusk,
By the infantine sadness of withdrawn grass courts,
By facades that did not know the plumb-line
—Seeming countenances with the irregular charm
Of the deep brow, the delicate mold—
Crests of this carapace
Carving great symmetries in space
Royalling out into harmonical whim
By arches that pull in the sky
Than that, having been braced by,
Having held onto
This profusion just made to blaze
Down the enormous perspectives of avenues
To the last of the barriers and borders,
It is to be enlarged by, to gain light from a mind,
It is to gain light from a world
Where, although we are poachers on these estates
(Ears ringing with the recounting of plots
Cabinets crowded with poisoned gloves)
It is irrelevant to question our rights to be here—
We have as much right as the caretaker's cat—
Irrelevant, too, to add that this is no legacy belonging to everyone—
For above all it was embellished
Like an unreasonable glory
Surging and twining in air,

Like an imaginary dwelling exciting belief,
Maintaining an expectation at full strength
In the tide of the hopes that drown
As the clouds come down to these storeys
And the sunset caught in the pinnacles
Still seems to be blowing bugles—
Heroical rumors, rumors!

Rain Song

My sad-bad rain that falls
In lisp and dibble-dabble
On the porch and under stairs
And puddles in the driveway brimmed
And dolloped by the slow loitering
Of the not-quite clapping hands
So slight they are on primrose
Leaves and the periwinkle
And keeps such babble going through the day.

Cats in beds sleep long
And I, I'd do the same
Or sing
If all the birds weren't gone.
It's silk under the elm leaves
It's slip into the streams
That clasp the globe around,
It's in the stealth to steal
Another tongue than bell
That does not strike but holds
All in its spell
So fresh and so small.

The Dominant House

At night it is that early history I walk
And it is to its flumes and woods I turn
Stealthily treading the winding back.
It is to the account of these in a wintry term
That I lay open the heart, the will disconnect,
It is for this that the bush of pink field
And the radiant and sombre star
Disentangle their crooked significance.
The last face of the moon over the North Meadow,
Cut up into pieces by the face of the leaves,
Now yellow and large and low-hung
Lays down a bolt of water-ribbed color
As the snapping of twigs in the wood meaning deer
The long lift of the wind to the pine bough
And the still-heard tones of the night-bird, insectivorous
Goat-sucker,
Ever singing from right to left to right
Never on the nearest bough,
Return to enter my thought.
How the voice of that mocker, distant,
Warms me in fancy. I lay my ear to its pure, unbroken voice
In the low bed where thinking is feeling is thinking
In the dominant house.
You, playing the piano,
Moths plunging in and out
Of the window that cats came through
Crazing after their company.
A peculiar reticence marking the weather
Some leaves were almost yellow
While others like an intelligent innocence

Where We Came

Where we came the grasses were high
And the flowers were openly lolling
Lilies in bank by the foxglove
Long shoots of forsythia that lay with the roses
Gone wild for the wasps to love.
It was all so vined and unhindered.
The flowers in their sum of blooming
Stood so close with the weeds that lived by the iris,
A covey of butterflies stooping
Just to the beardtongue.

Into what had we stumbled?
It all so belonged to them
As if between their colors and breaths
Some invisible thing had been woven
So hidden we could not have known
Had we come an instant more soon
Or should we stay, forever
Detained by their intricate languor.

The Water Wheel by the River Sorgue

Under this leaf-deep green
The water wheel turns and turns
I believe it is animated by another machinery,
Say, the voices of the cigales
As it turns and turns on the farm of waters
Where long-ribboned streamers of water plants lie
Just under the roof of the water
To make the clear water seem green not so.
Crazily creaking and hung in moss
It heaves itself round in a slow whirl
Of the flashings of chains of thin glitter
Hung from the rims and spokes.
Touched into motion that renews itself
It gains speed with the transports of four o'clock.
Then it is that the two form a capitol
Of the contagion of motion and sound.

As if in the fanfare of dream
How this great wheel turns in my head
Where I watch the treasures brought round each time
Of the dark moss and the chains of water
Until I am a trapper of cigales
Though I found at this center palaces
For the lean-bodied singers of the euphoria of summer
To continue their wiry notations
And clap my hands in applause
Of the pulsating orchestras

Until in the forever returning
Agitation of the overturned churning

And the ritardandos the water and moss would make
Though the gay din would have no delay
Voices other than their wiry ones
Seem to be drawn from out the commotion
Or from just under water or forth from recesses
Kept by the shadow of leaves and the cresses
Till I think every tongue of the summer's ages
Is given voice now that the wheel pours with
As it spins its own obbligato
And all is caught up in a crazy crescendo

Under such boughs as these
Where they sing in the arms of the trees
The innocent voices, keeping time
That the wheel beats to as it heaves around.

Have Driven in Carriages

Have driven in carriages, by violets traveled
In a field stolen over. In clear land what mist!
Of its long-bodied field blues flung in a heap—
Or the blur is of jewels or blush of cheeks, lips—
Seen from a distance where the air presses round,
Coloring the long-bodied heads in a group.
Nearby a sea wall. Clear panes of sea lifted,
Till the flash of the soft foam smokes.
Vinous roofs of the berry. A gardener strolling
High up in a heaven of straw for the oranges.
What presence contains us! You bearded!
Like that statue we saw embraced
By the rose grown over its brow.
Like azures to drink. The plane trees deep!
As, vagrant of pebbles, a pauper of leaves,
The snail delicately pulls in its horns,
Stopped by our carriage, our riding on fields,
Gone in to all that he is.

St. Sulpice

Morning: a still profoundness in the air
Shrouded with shreds and tatters of a silk
Of mist left standing in the boughs of trees
That pigeons wade through in a way of leaves
Sheared in the dark storm of the night before.
And one has come to sleeping lions here
Postured at the fountain for a drink
Of waters younger than the time we know
And somnolence of wet leaves and wet feet
Of birded morning in some temperance
Of dark facades, the regal ledge,
The half-cracked towers that rise upon the square
Like something that a pensive man has thought:
And on the porch blown feathers in a drift
For brides to walk in when the portals part.

Cracked Looking Glass

The tears, the firebursts and the vows,
The wild caprices and the bouts of pulse
The chills of sieged despairs, those flowers
Bought to match eyes and proffer aphrodisiacs
Of sighs and groans; the seizures.
World at the end of world when dusk falls slow
And all else but a taunting fast and loose.
Smooth skin, shut eyes and gliding limbs.

Love, I note you, stroke by stroke,
And show you how you play with shameless art
In the cracked looking glass that I hold up
What practice has made perfect, if it has.
The fits and starts, the going then to stay
The word, the gesture meant to take the heart
(If it be studied or be not)
Grand ceremonials of a play
By which we tried to live a passion out
By every nuance in a little room.
And cloistered so, tell out our stories
To pass the time until the moon rode high,
Improve upon the life we led,
Give gifts of praise, and so we did.
And if you postured in the looking glass
I made it for you, I held the witchery up
For you to see the secret life I guessed,
That more than improbable, celestial otherness.
And if you acted what I taught
Even as I learned it at your eyes
And your each ruse took on as if we borrowed

From every trick known to the over-wrought
And half-Platonic specialist,
We did it under moon craft or in twilight,
In all the half hours when the world becomes
All that imagination ever hoped it was.

My tear-quenched cost, I number half the ways
We chose a smoky vapor over fire
And tried to make a greater truth
Than what our contradictions could allow,
Exclaiming, as we breathed,
The true irrational.
And yet we were what we are.
And though the smoke is gone there is some fire
In saying so.

We made a play but not a discipline.
Love is the sternest master of the school.
But players tell a truth they cannot know.
They do not live it either, they enact
The fiery powers of instants in a light
Held up to them they cannot clarify.
Cease and be still. The pain is otherwise.
It's in the breaking face the clouds give to the moon
And in the flower that leans upon the air
Pouring its full life out into its scent.

Consecration Piece

Prince of that song, might I by some dark wine
No sovereign of the grape has ever crushed,
Drink to the sulky language of your tongue
That marred and yet unflawed so bends the string
To song that it would break with but does not
That whosoever hears must weep with love
That is yet strange with pain of deep delight
And weep as I do now, till wrung to bone
But then reprieved from that despair of vows
And not reluctant now, but eager, calm,
Thus is all so leaved and bound
Within such changeless measures, pledge
My life, if so I may, to those great staves
Clanging imperiously their star-solved sound.

Ballade

*"Oh! nos os sont revêtus d'un
nouveau corps amoureux"*—RIMBAUD

Vowing she had found again
What she would call the extreme and guiltless waters
Of which the soul might drink and body late
Sink into forgetfulness as into flowers,

She came to him she had elected, wild
As any artless and deceivèd child
Deceived by innocence nor reconciled
To the deep wounds love leaves unless it slays.

Her swift intemperance was the contagious ire
That stung his blood his mind might mock.
No matter that. The instant of the kiss
That seemed the balm had much the taste of truth

While the delicate *amor* of that fine ray
Sent from the beseechment of her eye
Skewered his heart; it twirled on the beam
Till in her eye he saw it spun again.

She was all lilied essence else
Of fields of France the lineaments
Who flaunted with the docile frowardness
Of unquestioned sovereigns a rare device,

A silken pennant with the words pricked out
To some such gold effect, he believed it read,
As love's new body that the bones put on.
The antique utterance flared round her head

As if the gold had sudden tongues of flame
Kindling the shadows till she seemed
(Or did a soaring fragrance dance them in?
Of strange surpassings that eluded him,)

Prodigious as the phoenix, yet of mien
Untouched as pearl, her arms of moon.
Thus guilelessly she entered all his senses
The while he put all dalliance away

To pace the mazes of her smile
And when she cried that they had come to that
Vision of the first bright shore
The body only has when it perceives

That other body of its soul,
He swore with her they had put on their bones
The luminous body of new love
At which the pennant fell she'd pinioned there

As a sign above their heads. It fell, they fell
Where particles of gold beset
Them in a penetration of the breast's most burning heat . . .

Then came the miserere of vows
The childish chorus of their enlacing cries
Reached to the heavens with a bird-like craze
And the embossed characters stood up more bright

Against the heraldic glister of that silk
They lay entented under, wound around,

Their senses roped in the intense profound
Where darkness backs on darkness in the ground.

And what is this? the angels might have said
Called forth star-like assailant, pitying

As if the bent bow might propel
Its raging arrow at the thing unknown
That touched, untouched, appears one instant then.
But platitudes his darling sang
Chanting of the new world they had found
Where might they live, die, live and rise again

As to the god whose freshness fired their room.
In that fire's freshness many a relic burned,
Keepsakes of past idolatries
Tossed in to get an incense from the mound

Where up they wind and dance to the hissing sound.
All else an exequy to this perfection found
Never before, they cried, untried, she prated then,
A year he lay with her out of the tomb.

Ah, but a year, and that device
Rots ten thousand times upon his breast.

As for the room wherein she tolled her lies
If it has not fallen into the spider's jaws—
And prays may no heart skewer in her eyes,
Not from her hands that innocence she dons

With each new love pull down upon
Pennant and words of such a bliss
As ends, he says, like this.
And damns her vows, those wailing cries,

Howled with the fire that leapt up from their words.
Trammeled by that, he founders, tented in red
Till all his bones char round him that he fed
For fumous incense to their spinning day.

First golden rays impale, then nails of ice!
And damns such stuff of time that brings such death
To those who trod like princes of the grass
That takes the westering moon and brooding stars

And all the world he rides from in hell's cars
(For still his senses sleep their miles away.)

   II
And now the angels would return
To pity and to warn again
This wound from half of Paradise he got.
For what seemed truth may rot

They said. Man loves in time and that's his shame
And what the stuff is that endures
We may but sing. And yet it is a ghostly thing.
Blest be the flesh that dreams its dream

And though it dreams no longer, dreams again
When trees put on their ribands of the red

By gravesides where they blossom fierily.
Then take your hearts from spite, they said.

For there's a ring of those who hate
Who neither die nor may beget,
Condemned to whirl without finality
Where no light is or fire in the thick ground.

And sang: You had a portion of all things:
Earth's music rolled, by the woods you came
From the dogsday den, shot by the moon's
Most wilding light. These powers we lent

And when you die they gather back what's spent.
Make silent hymn, then, to all element.
And sang: it is the madness then of man.
Blest be his madness though he wander blind.

Imperfect is his love and yet it reigns.
Until the sun divided by cloud bands,
The gold orb cut in two and then in three,
'Concluded and dropt down' and quenched their choirs

Which then the trees took up in leaving,
Blown out by autumn from some source
Of jubilant wisdom in the earth's body.

Little Ballad

The light of the stars pales the water
The willow lets down its leaves to drink
Morgan le Fay is not at home
Nor her ravens the daughters

But Sunday's child of grace is,
Close to the willow wren.
May I build you a house in the long leaves
Though the light's blown out by the wind?

Over the sleep-cast waters
Still and slowly flowing
May I bring you under the bridges
And by the locks where toil

The waters in loud repose
Where deep the trees in towers of leaves
The vine has cast on them, look in
To that still place in the stream?

I heard a young man say
To this gentlest one.
And then? she asked. And then?
Dark are the waters there,

Those waters draw the dream,
From there all currents run
As into the heartsblood
And may I bring you there

Past fields of sleep and grasses
Drowned at the water's brim?
And then? she asked, and then?
You looked at me and I am changed

And I shall love you long
If you love me. And if not—
What then? she cried, what then?

Each to His Dear Keeper Gone

Each to his dear keeper gone,
I paced the worn grounds thinking on
The eventful moment when our looks had crossed.
It seemed some wind had come and blown to me
By the exact lift of your glance or by your mouth
So sombre-sweet not time might sigh away
What love's faulty grace has blessed.
Yet in an instant you grow pale and far,
A doubleness besets you, for that other comes
With gliding stealth to put his own head on,
Cold player of the game! And yet it seems
Your own grows dearer by his shifty weight.
The impure thrives on the pure and that's a work
Much makes me fall between the tense of things
Into a warlock shuttling, too besought
By too much twining of the light and dark.
Memory, don't in your echo-chamber play too long
These mordents of the daggering theme
To which the dead gives obstinate counterpoint.

Written in London After a Protest Parade

Any messages, messages, any word?
Has the woman with her child gone home?
Has the Pole Anna, whose mother died,
Received good news? Is there a god?
And what of the gasman. Did he come?
The wind is high on this sea-blown isle
And it is tall in my room and dim.
At the shut window the curtains blow.
I don't want all that air. Don't let it in.
And the bulldog pup wrapped in a sweater
Whose obscene old grandmother barked at him,
Is he going to Brussels on the weekend?
His former father is a stud in Rome,
A most respectable pink-nosed pug,
And if he saw a bull would he bait him?

I walked with the women today, several abreast,
Escorted by policemen—"What a travesty!"
We set a fast pace and we had balloons
And black pennants on shepherd crooks
And ten or more trundled go-carts.
How the babies slept over their wheels
Up Kingsway through Ludgate Circus!
And at St. Paul's we waited an hour
To see a Masque and then it was over.

Any messages, messages, any word?
We were soluble in some concord,
For a while we were part of one
In an unproved, nearly abstract way.
Buttons were sold and *Peace News*,

We were 'on the side of humanity'
Herded by policemen, shot
By photographers every which way.
A goodly company of good will
Not bound to win but bound to try said one
With a face from which intelligence shone.
There were ministers' wives and a cold sun
On grimy St. Paul's with its swollen domes.

And what of the woman in the small back room
Who looked as young as her daughter?
She has stolen her daughter, in the same lumpy bed
Too narrow for one they slept together.
A sad intensity set them apart,
They were pale and still when I saw them.
And the wind. Will her husband come?
Will he send a bailiff or procure a judge?
She would know *what* to do if she knew *where*, she said.

Any messages, messages, any word?
Up in arms, at sea, tossed resistlessly
Almost at times not right in the head,
Opposing by erratic decisions what the heart only knows
After choice has canceled too late, too late,
Nursing the murderer there
Whether it hunts by knives
Or the thought that denies . . .
I am elated, but should we try
As some of us said, to die
If it comes to that, for what we believe?
If it *must* come to that, that is. . . .

Police of the Dead Day

I shall be a cat, pawing the streets,
A sunken beast with low-hung belly,
Himself discovered only in dark and the alley
In the dirt and the dark, turning corners
From the police of the dead day.
I shall be low like the cat, with the perverse taste
Of fishing for offal.
I shall find in the dark cellar groins profit,
There are those like me who even employ the moon
If the word *use* must be used again.
Ignorant of all but my skin, I may be skinned—
And it is possible for the sake of the pelt, alive—
But like those who have at last no choice
I in my penetrating voice
That arises from a deep local dislocation,
Will have put up my back against
Proctors production the regulation of fingers
That become taps, hands hooks by the indestructible
Engine whose production
Has nothing to do with the moon and my pupils that swell
With its swelling
Or that which goes on in the night and the hours
Between people actually living
Who for the moment have forgot that they must live by exploiting
Or the ghastly assumption, the dread difficulty of lying,
Who are nakedly trying for love,
Nakedly hurt, trying. . . .

Bleecker Street

Two infants vis-a-vis
Laughing, striking softly out
At one another in their carriage,
The American flag set out in bulbs—
The crookt stars and tawdry stripes,
Aren't they bizarre
To advertise a church bazaar
By backs of Spanish melons?
That child in the butcher shop
With lids so fine-cut over such a blue—
Inviolate—
Out of where?
O pure and neat, severe
Sentinel angel!
Life! Sister! A kitten sleeping
Ready to paw out if I scratch behind his ear!
I'm laden with your bread, your milk,
I'm thinking of you just the way
I'd think of lips, hair . . .
I'd sense like a kiss upon the cheek
The way you seem to be upon the air
Like one come from far
To favor us with careless smiles and blinks
Inscrutable!
But where the lamb hangs in his wool
I meet the waiter taking dinner
To my blind old neighbor,
Sick, blind, alone.
Yes, but we're disabled
To meet the many that you are,
You'd stifle us in backrooms of the soul!

There's no strutting we can do
Like my other neighbor's pigeons who've brought down
Some straw of snatched-up sunlight in their beaks.
Nothing that you do not contradict,
Our gentle, murderous Enigma!
And night comes round the corner after you. . . .

Of a Provincial City

In this foreign city there are two towns
One new, if not modern, of uninteresting buildings
And wide streets where abound many shops
Here you may think you are traveling
Meeting the new, experiencing something
Whatever it is it is really impossible to say.
And the crisp passersby, joined by your countrymen
And the middle class of every nation
Well-shaven, well-dressed, apt with the presumption
That whatever they want belongs to them.
It is private-public here
Though all's on display all is hidden
Except the supreme appearance of things
O how things live, how they exceed
And from their excess blows the brisk air of success
(It is the ease discomforts, the commonplace muffles—
That taste of brass in the mouth
From the invasion by locust hordes).

And there is the other town full of bicycles
Crooked of streets, broken of sidewalks
Where hotel rooms smell of insecticide
Such rooms have no views save on dead ends
That cats, drunk on sex, consort in.
Monsieur le patron has a caged bird
Who makes loop the loops when he is not talking
With the broken voice of a crow child.
Madame sweeps the room of the spiders left
From somebody's nightmare. On streets like this
Girls hang around on Saturday night with such intricate towers of hair

They charge nicely to climb up in.
Old women in mourning. *Velos* and *Motos*.
A square filled with a fair, if you will,
Of wool underwear and cheap pants.
The hot tasting breath from bakeries . . .

Here they are not unlike their cats sitting at doors.
They have raised the shade of their plane trees
Under which they play bowls. In cafés card games,
The *relais* of lovers.
And the hale meeting of men in broad brims.
Here what it is seems what it is.
Not altogether for sale.
Everyone is living, yes, by the other
In the elaborate network of exchanging
Labor for idleness. But idleness is also provisioned for
And they spend it freely.
Of the grand fanfare they are a part.
They need not flee always to the benches, the bleachers.
If they cheat you they do it without palaver.

And in some ancient court of honor
You may come across a statue
Wearing a vest of thick moss.
A voice still coils from the murmuration
Of a fountain and here are bees laden with pollen
From flowers a wind has transported from Greece.
O stiff stubborn purity of that head
On whose lips a bee settles
Drowsing in sun from his airy labors awhile. . . .

Nth Invitation

Let us live in a warehouse with green-blinded shutters
Where I will store like stuffed owls my griefs
And keep an old barge nearby.
Let the shape of the building be like this—but I cannot draw—
With a hook at the top for hoisting up
Whatever has fallen headfirst below.
You have heard of my recipes for divination before
But do you know of my simpler pleasures?
How I would bake oysters or roast eggs in a trunk jammed with hay
And to what I am committed when at evening windows slantly contend
     with skies
As the rivers like so many green arms ride up to meet the canals
Under the fiats laid down by the boughs
And it is no accident, it was planned that way
And it is guarded, this *belle* harmony,
Both so civilized and instinctual, so airy and grave
That it steadies and strengthens our frayed resolves.

And will you not understand
That when I fling open these cuckoo doors
To the hard edifices outside
Of our doubtful legacies and our dear dead god
I am thinking, too, of those turning the other cheek
To the Founders of State,
And the long prisons for those who will not quit the vision
Of what they have truly learned
Burns like time's face in the tower's clock.

Das Wort des Teufels

Clear light on a brass world
Where cars outlaw the idle saunterers.
Not that they do, but no one's here.
Their racket drives good thoughts away.
The weeds themselves stand much in dust.
It is the itch of seekless stir,
It is the phlegm of weight, the tar's enclosure,
It is loss for the snail horns
It is not seeing an old coat on the back of a nag
Nor the dense verdure of that blue-green
Walking by night in expectations lived by day
If the soul comes home to sleep at night at all
After they have gone back into their blue-painted air.

Passive against the spurt of engines
The backfire bursts of venom,
The little exhaust pipe spitting out
Like something in a medieval legend.
Das Wort des Teufels. Money.
I walk the grimly sun-lit Sunday street.
Nobody but birds and me. The gears are smashed
That gave me license. It is my license
To avoid the gears.
                    Hearing the news of weather
From screen doors. Petunias keep it up
By shabby alleys.
And marigolds, hedged in by Lilliputian fences.

To disencumber the world of these machines.
Am I hard and unloving to our general state?
Must its abusings be forgiven
Because what is is what we must accept?
'Minds beaten thin by waste.'

Suite

Afterwards (JULY 15, 1964)

Debts writing me letters,
Mice running under my bed,
My mother's horse looks in the door,
Her fingers waltz the window pane.

O that piano in the Alps.
Louder it swells, again, again!
I wake. The moon is shining in.
Its stains are on the floor, a chair.
The smashed white clock she cannot mend again.

Nota Bene

I'll break your heart, A. said to me
You'll break my heart, I said to B.
Both did, and still, is my ticker all that smashed?
We get over old wounds by acquiring new ones,
Said C. And thus I obtained all three.

Your Words

Your words cross back from days
I try to think just when it was
You said that beautiful thing
Or chiseled that flamboyant phrase

And thinking am half lost
In pursuit again
Of how it was you looked
When your painted speeches shook
My reluctant heart.

The Beginning

You
Came drifting up to me
As a cat will seek a new home
When a summer master's left.
And I was charmed by that,
I did not ponder riddles, I esteemed
The surfaced play, the light
Inconsequential thing
And wished to be a matchfire for a moth.

And the Platonic Order

And the Platonic order of the morning, chaste,
Spontaneous, with a hot cool sun
The satin cups of the crocus, the hyacinth
Not Greek, not "ensanguined with woe,"
Already the loose knot of violets
Lead me. And I cannot go.

Again, Again

Always that old language for the new:
How many eyes are black or brown or blue.
How many have come naked into bed
The curtains drawn; late morning that lets in
Just so much light to gild the rose-gold head.
That amorini look—intent and bent
To fast desire on nothing else but it
A century long.
How many times. How many arms
How many kisses that the gamblers gave
Or pitched all on to win
Or gaining win to lose again.
How many times. And now you come.
Have cigarettes, cigars, guitars and rum!
How many times! Yet none but this—
So sighing lovers sigh in their excess
To have the heart unlettered in its breast,
Unlettered of all histories but this,
This last be first and none but this!

The Flux of Autumn

All is a golden burst, the wind burning
The golden trees that plunge
Headmost into the burning light and make
A sound as fierce as waterfalls—
Excitable air of dying changes,
Autumn of the year and of the height!

So I by Shady walking saw old leaves
Whirled in hardy rings and circles plunged,
Gyration of the fire-plagued spirits crying!
And saw it was a fight to the death this year,
The fortress mountains thinning their own shapes,
Advancing now from thickets of the sense,
From wayward, tall, exultant, sap-choked green,
A hardy brambled green that founders us,
Into this umbre, sombre, earth-dark thing
That then at twilight imitates a blue
And in a link, a series, and a bare earth-warded
Chain sets up the gaunter distances
Between their star-reefed differences and us.

What is this dream we make with leaf-rained earth
Or do we live upon a fire not ours
Like absentees of will, Undines of fantasies
Waiting and listening in a rich suspense
Expecting half our dreams to be its selves
And all of what we love our own?
So then the reddening apple is as much germane
And those tuft-headed grasses of the field
Rising above their lower-lying kin

And how they are is how they stand
Leaning upon the wind that moves the mind
To lean upon the same all-mothering stuff
And draw the intricate world more close

Until we'd think the rudest empire of tough chaff and rock
The very form of our subjective wish
Reshaped again within the restless eye
That takes its bearings from the true itself
To enter then on changes of its being,
A changeless changing, transformings into
An ethereal storming, freshening, continuous,

For I have heard those voices rough
As shaggy earth and humming with the earth's own tilth
Or mad as water hurled against a stone
So now you remnant butterfly whose motion makes
A silent music, repeat, repeat,
And you thin clouds who deepen in the skies
Your soundlessness against the surged uproar
Until the four winds seem to swell one tone
From out the banter between field and wood
To let us think all things are full of gods.

As shadow falls upon a rock.
The shadow of a bird has crossed my heart
That we are these, these living things, enough!
By them we make a burning territory
Wherein there walk those influences of sky
At that long moment of the eye

When all leaps upward at some ancient wind
Blown from the corners of some leaf-blocked road
We walk upon in sober truth. To be so caught
By all this phantomed streaming forth
It seems a greater phantom is at work.

Quick-shading now, the battle of leaves,
The airy-quick, a gusty lunging, throbbing,
Metallic clangor, pipes, the errant horn.
Misled by fevers then, by ditches lost,
By fireweed and the hawks that plunge,
This that I'm in's become a changeling cloud.
The clarity of mountains is obscured
By what we'd fortify that must be dreamed.
Old territory mapped and walked
Nightly, daily, in the impetuous eye
Of thought.
                    Until the dream's walked out.